Thom & Joani Schultz

KIDS TAKING CHARGE:

Youth-Led Youth Ministry

By
Thom and Joani Schultz

Loveland, Colorado

Kids Taking Charge: Youth-Led Youth Ministry
Copyright © 1987 and 1991 Group Publishing, Inc.
First Printing, 1991
This book was originally published as *Involving Youth in Youth Ministry*.

Designed by Judy Bienick
Cover designed by Dori Walker
Cover photograph by David Priest
Scripture quotations in this book are from the *Good News Bible*, the Bible in Today's English Version. Copyright © American Bible Society 1966, 1971, 1976. Used by permission.

Library of Congress Cataloging-in-Publication Data
Schultz, Thom
    [Involving youth in youth ministry]
    Kids taking charge : youth-led youth ministry / by Thom and Joani Schultz
      p.   cm.
    ISBN 1-55945-078-9
    1. Church work with youth. 2. Youth—Religious life.
  I. Schultz, Joani Lillevold, 1953-   . II. Title.
  BV4447.S36   1991
  259' .23—dc20   91-36115
                                            CIP

Printed in the United States of America

——

*T*his book is dedicated to Angie, Chinh, Chris, Deb,
Gara, John, Judy, Mike, Rick and Tom—the kids
on our church's youth-based planning task force and first
steering committee, who inspired us to write this book.

Table of Contents

Table of Charts

CHAPTER ONE

The Case for Involving Youth in Youth Ministry

O ur youth group needed a transfusion.
For years it had centered around the youth pastor or adult sponsors. Some successes here and there. But the youth ministry had grown as much as it could under the current system. And the adult leaders were tired and burning out.

Dozens of great kids attended our church. But dozens stayed away whenever we planned anything. And most of the stuff we planned was pretty good.

We began to listen to the kids:

"The youth group is boring."

"I don't like any of the kids who go to the youth group."

"We never do anything I want to do."

"I wish the group would be like it was five years ago.

This church had a great youth group back then."

"I'd rather go to the youth group at my friend's church."

A New Start

We decided to get radical. We shut down the whole high school youth ministry program.

Pastor Dan Hansen, Joani and I sensed our kids would welcome a change. A vote by the existing group validated our hunch. The group selected several kids to serve on a team to redesign the youth ministry.

Four months later, a new youth ministry began to emerge. And since then, the kids and the entire youth ministry at our church have bloomed. The youth group is an even more tightly knit family. Kids care more for one another. The majority of our church's young people are involved in the youth ministry program. The kids themselves run much of the program. They plan every meeting, lead the activities, teach many of the lessons, prepare the publicity and chart the long-term plans.

Previously shy, quiet kids now take part in leadership roles with surprising self-assuredness. All of the kids are learning decision-making skills that surely will help them in years to come.

The kids' faith has deepened. Their commitment to the church has strengthened.

Now we overhear kids telling their friends, "We have the best youth group in town."

This book is the story of youth-based ministry. It's a guided tour through a youth ministry approach that developed over years of "hard knocks." In the early '70s, when we began implementing the elements of what we now call youth-based ministry, Joani and I were working in different states and didn't even know each other.

But we shared a common belief that high-school-age young people are a capable species. We believed that youth ministry could be something more than another spectator sport for kids. We observed that young people learned more, developed more and grew closer to God when they moved from being passive youth ministry spectators to active doers.

We took some risks. Suffered some embarrassing moments. But over the years, the young people themselves proved the viability of youth-based ministry.

A New Approach

In 1977, GROUP Magazine initiated its national workcamp mission program. And the youth-based ministry approach has characterized these workcamps from the start. At these weeklong events, crews rebuild homes of needy families. Five young people and one adult comprise each crew. We entrust the young people with a great deal of responsibility and decision-making. Each crew member assumes a specific role and responsibility for the week. For instance, one person is the "quartermaster," who is responsible for the necessary tools. Another is the "reporter," who communicates with the base camp concerning what has been accomplished and what additional materials and tools are needed. Another is the "work director," who makes on-site task assignments and keeps the project moving.

Traditional youth ministry philosophy dictates that the adult should be the work director. That's often not the case at a GROUP workcamp. A 15-year-old kid may have more construction experience than the adult crew member. So the kid directs the work while the adult takes care of the tools. That may be humbling and uncomfortable for the adult. But the young work director's self-esteem soars. And the work is accomplished with surprising quality.

Some adults accept this youth-based structure at the workcamps. Some do not.

I remember speaking with an adult who attended GROUP workcamps two consecutive years. He said, "This year's experience with the kids on my crew was sure a lot different than last year's. Last year I thought my role was to tell the kids what to do. After all, construction supervision is my profession! Well, last year we got the work done all right. But I don't think the kids learned much. They just quietly followed my orders.

"This year, I decided to try it your way. A kid from Michigan was our work director. He did a good job. Once in a while, he asked for my advice, which was neat. Most work decisions were talked over and made by the crew as a whole. By the middle of the week, the crew was working great. We got the job done, but more importantly, those kids really grew! They loved the week! They really felt they made a difference.

"Last year, I didn't even take time out for the crew devotions. I considered that was a waste of time when there was so much work to do. But this year I encouraged the girl who served as the crew's devotions leader. She did a great job. By the end of the week, the kids really made the connection between their work and Christ's call to serve—even 'unto the least of these.' "

That adult caught the vision of youth-based ministry.

I hope that you too will catch the vision of youth-based ministry. Joani and I are thoroughly convinced that the youth worker's primary role is to involve *youth* in their own youth ministry. May the following pages help you to help your young people become all that they can be as full members of the body of Christ.

—*Thom Schultz*

CHAPTER TWO

The Benefits and Dangers of Youth-Based Ministry

*T*he kids on the planning task force had been working for months on the new youth ministry structure for the church. The team decided to reveal its radical new approach to the parents first. The adults on the planning task force affirmed this decision. "Parents are really key to the success of this approach to youth ministry," said one of the adults. "Would you want the pastor or me to present our ideas to the parents?"

The kids nervously glanced at each other.

Finally, one of the guys said, "Ah, how about having us present this stuff to the parents?"

The adults nervously glanced at each other.

"Well, ah, sure," the pastor said. "I guess that would really demonstrate our new approach in action."

So, the kids divided up the responsibilities for the parents meeting.

On the night of the big meeting, the pastor and other adult leaders gulped and whispered to one another. "I hope this comes off okay," said one, "or we're gonna have a pack of angry parents who think we've shirked our responsibilities and have allowed these kids to get in over their heads."

The pastor called the meeting to order, welcomed the parents, and said, "Tonight's meeting will be presented by the young people."

The parents nervously glanced at each other.

The meeting came off well—very well, in fact. Each young person had prepared well and did a fine job explaining this new concept called youth-based ministry. Some of the parents were skeptical about the new approach. But all were quite impressed with the kids' confident presentation.

The parents and adult sponsors saw that the young people were capable of wielding significant responsibility. And the kids themselves saw that they could do it. They believed in themselves.

What Is It?

Youth-based ministry is a ministry *for* young people— operated largely *by* young people.

Young people themselves do most of the planning, preparing and executing for youth ministry programs, activities and service missions. Selected young people plan youth group meetings and special events. They decide on the content and how to pull it off. They delegate to the other young people the responsibilities for directing games and crowdbreakers, song leading, praying and leading Bible studies and discussions to other young people. The kids do the publicity; make many of the youth ministry's financial decisions; handle disciplinary problems within the group; and plan and prepare lock-ins, retreats and trips. They're in charge of setting goals and shaping the future of youth ministry in the church.

In addition to carrying much of a youth ministry's workload, the kids learn decision-making skills. They constantly are faced with weighing the pros and cons of various choices that will affect their futures.

What about the adults' role in youth-based ministry? They're still active. Their job is no easier; in fact, it's more challenging. On first glance, youth-based ministry appears to relieve the adult leaders of much of their responsibility. "Hey, the kids are doing it all. We can sit back and relax," you might say. What's not so apparent is the adults' ever-present behind-the-scenes work. Without that, youth-based ministry quickly fizzles. Casual observers, and even the young people themselves, seldom notice or appreciate all the silent supportive work that adults contribute to youth-based ministry.

Paid youth workers and volunteer sponsors must be willing to relinquish much of the leadership spotlight—to allow the kids to perform in its glow. And to suffer in the spotlight when the performance is less than good.

Young people are the visible doers. Adults are the humble servants. Adults are involved in youth ministry, not for their own glory, but to satisfy a Christlike craving to see young people grow to be all they can be as God's children.

You should note at this point that the principles and the experiences described in this book refer to youth ministries with high-school-age young people. While many aspects of youth-based ministry will function with younger kids, best results seem to come with high-school-age kids. Their more advanced maturity allows them to weigh tough issues, make difficult decisions, deal with setbacks and failures, and accept heavier responsibilities.

The Benefits of Youth-Based Ministry

Youth-based ministry delivers many advantages. Some are obvious. Some are subtle. Let's look at a few.

Benefit 1: Youth ownership of youth ministry. Mike was a very marginal member of the youth group. He showed up whenever he thought there might be some nice-looking girls present. He couldn't be counted upon to fulfill any significant responsibility—until he saw that his input and decisions actually affected the landscape of the youth ministry at our church. Thereafter he rarely missed a meeting or activity, he volunteered to do extra work, and he became the youth ministry's chief spokesperson during announcement time at Sunday morning worship.

Why the change in Mike's behavior? Because he realized that the youth ministry at his church was *his*. Not the pastor's. Not Thom's. Not Joani's. Not the youth board's. His.

When we own something, we take a heightened interest in it. Take, for instance, your home or car. Chances are, you're willing to invest more of your time, energy and money in your own house or car than you would a rental.

Young people are no different. When they realize they are the shapers of the youth ministry, they perceive they've been given the deed of ownership. As owners, they're more likely to participate. And that means better chances for increased attendance.

Youth commitment often soars. We remember Wendy. Before the advent of youth-based ministry in our church, she rarely showed an interest in youth ministry activities. She always said, "I have to work." Then, interestingly, the other kids elected her to the new steering committee.

She took on the responsibility of building community in our group—mixers, games and get-acquainted activities. She began attending youth group meetings regularly. She sensed she was needed. She knew that if she did not prepare a community-building experience for a given week, that it would not get done.

Every week Wendy would troop into the meeting with a roll of toilet paper, 3×5 cards or some other zany prop for an experience that would help draw us closer together as the body of Christ. We looked forward to Wendy's time in the spotlight.

The whole group counted on her to do the job, and to do it well. And she did. Because it mattered. She mattered. The group mattered.

When young people take ownership of a group, they tend to stick around. They're a part of it. They're needed.

Benefit 2: Life skills training. Youth-based ministry teaches young people valuable life skills through active learning experiences. They learn responsibility. They collect self-esteem when they follow through with a task; they know the whole group is counting on them. And they discover the painful consequences of shirking responsibility; things fall apart. No one may rescue them.

Youth-based ministry teaches decision-making skills. Young people learn to examine all sides of an issue, weigh the pros and cons, forecast outcomes, explore alternatives. They learn the process of applying Christian principles to everyday situations.

One of our groups struggled over what to do with an extra $500 in the treasury. Fund-raising projects for the upcoming summer trip had been more successful than anticipated. "Now, what shall we do with the money?" we asked the kids. Several suggestions surfaced:

1. Reduce the amount each person was required to pay

for the trip.

2. Cover the registration fees for two kids who were having trouble coming up with the money.

3. Keep the money in the treasury as a "nest egg" for next year's trip.

4. Add a stop at an amusement park to the trip.

5. Donate the money to help fight world hunger.

A heated discussion ensued. Advantages and disadvantages were shared for each plan. The kids decided to use the money to help the two low-income kids. What a great lesson in Christian stewardship! What a wonderful experience in authentic decision-making!

Young people also learn about leadership and organization. They discover—by doing—what works with people and what doesn't.

And they learn something about discipline. They discover the need for rules and guidelines. They grapple with fair consequences for those who break the rules. (Adults learn that young people who help make the rules are far less likely to break them. Especially if they know their peers may dish out the punishment.)

Benefit 3: Enhanced self-worth and personal growth. Youth-based ministry supplies kids with a commodity they crave during adolescence: self-esteem.

After a youth-led parents meeting, we asked 15-year-old Mark for his reaction. "I like speaking in front of the parents," he said. "It makes me feel good—like I'm important or something."

A few months later, Mark's family moved out of state. But before he left, we took him out for dinner. There he told us about his turbulent childhood. His mother and father had divorced when he was 10. He said his out-of-state mother really didn't care to see him anymore. And life with his father and stepmother was difficult. And now he faced uprooting again, moving away from the few friends he'd made.

"I'm gonna miss everybody here," he said, pausing to chomp on an ice cube. "But you know what I'm really gonna miss? The youth group. I mean, just look at all the plans we've made. I worked really hard on that stuff. But, you know, I didn't mind the work. 'Cause it seemed like the more I put into the group, the more I got out of it. I could see that what I was doing was helping the group grow. That makes me feel good.

"I don't want to leave. This is the first time in my life where I've been a part of something where I think I really have made a difference."

Mark's response to youth-based ministry was more candid than most. But the growth that took place in Mark is quite common.

Adolescence is a time of identity formation. During the teen years, people make significant conclusions about themselves. And since adolescent self-concepts are often tenuous, many young people form rather negative images of themselves. Parents, teachers and youth workers often demand that teenagers act like adults, but rarely are adolescents granted adult-level privileges and responsibilities. So, these "emerging adults" often feel undefined, mistrusted and underestimated.

Now, along comes youth-based ministry. Young people are given significant doses of real responsibility. Adults stop and listen to the kids' ideas. The kids themselves make most of the decisions. They feel the accomplishment of a job well-done. And they feel the deflation of a group failure.

Over time, adolescents' self-confidence builds through their involvement in youth-based ministry. After Wendy led games and mixers for a couple of months, her tentative shyness melted into self-assured leadership. Mike's weak announcements in front of the whole congregation soon became the polished (and quite entertaining) work of a self-confident young man.

Youth-based ministry provides a fertile environment for fostering kids' positive self-esteem. And a positive self-image enables young people to grow confidently as Jesus' disciples. To share their faith; to make tough moral choices in the face of peer pressure; to care for the outcast.

Benefit 4: Broad distribution of work. Youth-based ministry distributes the work to many people. The youth worker is no longer looked upon as ringleader, lion tamer, trapeze artist, clown and custodian. Everyone shares in the tasks of running a successful youth ministry. Kids, volunteer youth workers, parents and professional staff all contribute in significant ways.

Our group decided to plan a summer bike trip through Yellowstone National Park. Ordinarily, the youth pastor would make all the plans for such a trip. But, under the new youth-based ministry, the kids planned the trip. They split up the responsibilities. Some researched the route. Others planned the menu. Others arranged for camping equipment. And others scheduled local bike hikes to get the group into shape.

Spreading the workload frees the key youth ministry adult leadership to watch over the big picture and to ask, continually, the important questions: Are our young people growing closer to Christ? Is their faith making a difference in their everyday lives? Are they learning the basic Christian lifestyles of servanthood, compassion, love and humility?

Delegation of work is a central concept of youth-based ministry.

Benefit 5: Youth ministry continuity. GROUP Magazine research shows that professional youth workers stay at a church an average of three years. Turnover of volunteer youth workers is more frequent.

Under traditional youth ministry structures, this turn-over often results in upheaval among the young people. If the departing youth worker was the key person, planner, speaker, teacher, organizer and up-front talent, the youth ministry usually unravels shortly after his or her departure. Why? Because the youth ministry was built largely on his or her strengths. When he or she leaves, few strengths remain.

We've seen this happen more often than we care to count. Churches love to hire razzle-dazzle youth workers. Typically, they attract kids like moths to light. Kids adore them. These attractive leaders regrettably become the focus of the youth ministry. When they leave (and most of them *do* leave within three years) they take their ministry with them. The kids are left to flounder.

But in youth-based ministry, the youth worker is *not* the focus of the youth ministry. The strength of the program lies within the young people and a corps of caring adult volunteers. So, when the youth worker eventually moves on, the ministry continues. Sure, the youth worker and his or her gifts will be missed. There will be an important gap to fill. But the ministry shouldn't fall apart. The kids won't let it. They know the "secrets" to a successful youth ministry. And they're equipped to keep up the momentum.

Benefit 6: Provides a good model for the whole congregation. What's God dream for the church? Is it that a bunch of people pool their money, hire a minister, and then tell this minister to do God's work while they stand back and watch? We don't think so. That would be too akin to an underworld figure hiring a "hit man" to do the dirty work.

Jesus didn't say, "Go out and hire someone to feed my sheep." The ministry of the church was never sup-

posed to be sublet. But somehow many churches today
have confined the work of the ministry to a few paid
professionals.

Ministry is everybody's job. Youth-based ministry
exemplifies this Christlike approach. And it's contagious
in congregations. Members see the young people taking
active responsibility for their ministry. Then people of all
ages within the church often begin to take their roles
more seriously as ministers.

Youth-based ministry helps to promote the concept that
we are all ministers, not merely spectators.

Benefit 7: Enhanced youth evangelism. Most of us
became followers of Christ through a series of relationships. And, most of the non-Christian teenagers who will
come to the faith this year will do so as a result of a relationship with a Christian friend or family member. Larry
Keefauver, in his book *Friends & Faith* (Group Books),
noted these findings of how people become part of Christian communities:

- .01 percent through evangelistic crusades,
- 1 percent through church visitation,
- 4 percent through church programs,
- 4 percent through a pastor or simply by walking in,
- 70 to 90 percent through the invitation of a friend.

As Keefauver says, "The conclusion is simple. Friends
bring friends to Christ." Youth-based ministry encourages
and empowers young people to let their light shine. They
come to realize that attracting new kids to the church and
to Christ is not the job of Pastor Bob; it's their job.

Benefit 8: Increased youth visibility. In the youth-
based ministry model, a church's young people become
more visible. They're up front doing the youth announcements on Sunday morning. They're the key players in
the evangelism efforts to attract new members. They're
involved at every level of youth ministry planning and

doing.

Families frequently select a new church based on the church's concern for its youth. Churches using the youth-based ministry model showcase their commitment to youth.

The Dangers of Youth-Based Ministry

Thus far we've portrayed a pretty sweet picture of youth-based ministry. But it's not all rosy. There are definite drawbacks. And you should be aware of them before reading further.

Danger 1: Youth-based ministry is less streamlined than leader-based ministry. Youth-based ministry often seems unwieldy and cumbersome. Youth workers new to this philosophy often say, "It is faster and easier if I just do it myself." Usually they're right.

Before you may have been able, by yourself, to plan a youth group meeting in 30 minutes. Now you're helping the kids plan it. Instead of just putting it together, you're having to present options for them to choose from. Instead of feeding them material you have prepared, you are supplying them with resources and letting them lead the meeting.

With youth-based ministry, more people are involved in the process. And that usually results in a slower process in comparison to one person who does most everything.

Danger 2: A higher failure factor. When young people are doing tasks usually done by adults, the chances for failure may be higher. Last year, the kids in our youth group voted to plan a big fall retreat. They set the dates and paid a substantial deposit to a retreat center. But they overlooked one "little" detail: The dates they picked for the retreat coincided with homecoming and state tennis finals, activities in which many of them were involved. The retreat had to be canceled, and the deposit was forfeited.

Kids aren't adults. They don't have the benefit of vast experience. They will make mistakes. They will forget important deadlines. They will fail.

The senior pastor and the congregation may, if not properly educated, misinterpret the group's failures. "What are we paying our youth worker for?" they may ask. "That youth group has had three bombs in a row. It's embarrassing. Has our youth worker just turned over *all* responsibilities to the kids and checked out?"

Youth-based ministry can be risky, especially if the congregation hasn't been properly trained to understand apparent failures. A congregation must be trained to support young people (and adults) in their failures, so that everyone can learn and grow.

Danger 3: Adults who will not "buy into" a youth-based approach. This form of youth ministry isn't for everyone. Some adults find it too uncomfortable. And these people—both professional youth workers and volunteers—can make youth-based ministry most unpleasant. They seem to fall in three general categories:

First, we have the "star" leader. This individual loves the attention that young people send his way. He "needs" to be up front leading songs, performing in goofy skits, speaking and leading prayers. When asked to allow young people to take over some of these responsibilities, he bristles and balks.

Next, we have the "dictator" leader. She believes that young people need an authority figure. It's her job to tell the kids what to do, and it's the kids' job to obey. She makes the decisions and tells the kids what to believe. The concept of teaching kids *how* to decide is just too foreign for her. In her black-and-white world, youth-based ministry seems almost non-Christian.

Then, we have the "detached" leader. This one really likes the sound of youth-based ministry. "Great! Let's let the kids do it," he says. "Then we can just sit back and watch." When the kids fumble a responsibility, the detached leader flares with anger. "What's wrong with those kids? They're so irresponsible! They're acting like a bunch of kids!" He doesn't want to accept the notion that the adults' role in youth-based ministry is ·an active one.

Youth-based ministry requires understanding adults who love kids, who trust them to make good decisions, and who are willing to risk with them.

Anyone contemplating youth-based ministry must weigh the dangers and pitfalls of this approach. It most assuredly is not the easiest form of youth ministry administration.

But then, things of value rarely come easily.

A Scriptural Basis for Youth-Based Ministry

Youth-based ministry is scripture-based. It takes Jesus' example of leadership seriously. For example, notice how Jesus used some of the most unsuspecting people on his team. A fisherman or two; a tax collector; a political activist; himself, a carpenter. All volunteers by anyone's standards. Yet Jesus believed in his troupe. He knew they could do it—even when they doubted.

To make youth-based ministry work, you must follow Jesus' model of leadership for the kids. You need to . . .

● **Give away responsibility.** Jesus said, "What you prohibit on earth will be prohibited in heaven, and what you permit on earth will be permitted in heaven. And I tell you more: whenever two of you on earth agree about anything you pray for, it will be done for you by my Father in heaven. For where two or three come together

in my name, I am there with them'' (Matthew 18:18-20).
Jesus didn't say, "I'm the only one qualified to be in
ministry, so I'll just do it all.'' Instead, he said, in effect,
"I'll trust *you* to do it. Then I can be multiplied and
everyone will grow.''

● **Challenge kids.** You must challenge them to do
more than they think they can. Remember Peter's water-
walk adventure (Matthew 14:22-33)? Jesus modeled an
incredible feat and believed Peter could do the same.
Youth-based ministry challenges; it expects kids to learn
by doing, following their leaders' example.

● **Pick kids up when they fail.** Back to Peter's
walk on the water. What if you expect the most from
kids—and they bomb? Like Jesus, you can't stand back
and let them drown. Hold on to them tightly and pick
them up. One failure doesn't mean they won't be able to
start anew. Look at Peter! "And so I tell you, Peter: you
are a rock and on this rock foundation I will build my
church, and not even death will ever be able to overcome
it" (Matthew 16:18).

● **Believe in young people.** Imagine Jesus' trust in
his disciples when he sent them to get the word out.
"Jesus called the twelve disciples together and gave them
power and authority to drive out all demons and to cure
diseases. Then he sent them out to preach the Kingdom
of God and to heal the sick" (Luke 9:1-2). Believe that
your group members and adults can do great things. Because they can.

● **Stick together.** "And I will be with you always, to
the end of the age" (Matthew 28:20). Even if you're not
physically by their side, you can support your kids. Encourage them with phone calls, notes, prayers. Let your
group know you're a team. You're in this together.

● **Avoid burnout.** There is something particularly sad-
dening about a burned-out pastor or other church leader.

Regardless of whose "fault" it is for their condition, these leaders' exhaustion, bitterness and pain are often visible to the congregation. Youth workers are certainly vulnerable to burnout. Youth-based ministry steers leaders away from burnout by distributing the work.

Remember Moses' burnout? He had become overwhelmed with his workload. He cried to the Lord: "Why have you given me the responsibility for all these people? I didn't create them or bring them to birth! Why should you ask me to act like a nurse and carry them in my arms like babies all the way to the land you promised to their ancestors? Where could I get enough meat for all these people? They keep whining and asking for meat. I can't be responsible for all these people by myself; it's too much for me! If you are going to treat me like this, have pity on me and kill me, so that I won't have to endure your cruelty any longer" (Numbers 11:11-15).

God told Moses to find 70 people to help him in his leadership responsibilities. God knows the value of shared leadership.

● **Trust the Holy Spirit.** Remember Jesus' promise: "If you love me, you will obey my commandments. I will ask the Father, and he will give you another Helper, who will stay with you forever" (John 14:15-16). That promise holds true for your group. God's Spirit is present. "The Spirit's presence is shown in some way in each person for the good of all" (1 Corinthians 12:7).

Youth-based ministry affirms the power of God's Spirit working in people of any age. We remember Rick making an earnest plea for additional funds for the youth group mission trip. As he spoke to the congregation, he wasn't speaking alone. The Spirit touched hearts through him, a 17-year-old young man. After that day, the group had the money they needed for their mission adventure.

In addition to Jesus' style of leadership, the Bible gives

another concrete message that applies to youth-based ministry: "All of you are Christ's body, and each one is a part of it" (1 Corinthians 12:27). The church, Christ's body, makes use of *all* its parts. Young people won't be the church someday. They're the church right now. And with leaders exercising and toning the body's young muscles, the church will be in healthy condition.

Youth-based ministry. This is youth ministry by faith. And that is good.

CHAPTER THREE

Evaluating Your Present Youth Ministry

F requent evaluation—of self and ministry—is an essential practice. Your practice of evaluation demonstrates your willingness to grow. It provides an honest look at what could be improved upon, and it offers a chance to celebrate the good things.

Right now is a good time to look at your youth ministry from a fresh perspective. Look at the big picture. Are your young people steadily growing closer to Christ? Are they making a difference in the lives of others? Does your youth ministry attract new families to your church? Does your youth ministry in some way touch the lives of all the kids in your church? (For example, a youth ministry based on a youth choir is not a complete ministry.)

When we say, "Evaluate!" we're not expecting you to trash everything you're currently doing. In the youth-

based ministry model, many good aspects of your current
youth ministry may continue, with little or no change.

To determine if youth-based ministry is right for you
and your church, we recommend evaluating your current
situation from several perspectives. Each of the following
sets of people should be involved in the evaluation process: young people (including currently uninvolved kids),
parents of teenagers, adult volunteer sponsors, church
staff, and you as the key person.

Evaluation by the Young People

We target our youth ministries for young people. It's
sensible then that they should be key evaluators of our
efforts. But so often we've seen youth ministries that go
for years without ever asking the kids for their opinions.
Instead, the adults theorize and draw conclusions on their
own without going to the source. That's like trying to determine what childbirth is like, so you ask everyone in the
delivery room—except the mother.

It is dangerous to make assumptions about young
people's reactions to our youth ministry efforts. Youth
ministry speaker Rich Van Pelt took part in a large,
weeklong conference of high-school-age young people a
couple of years ago. Many gifted communicators shared
their presentations with thousands of kids. Then, toward
the end of the week, a high-school-age girl spoke to the
crowd about her own personal experience. Rich felt sorry
for her as she stammered and stumbled through her
speech. She looked especially unpolished compared to the
professional speakers who shared the platform that week.
But her message came from her heart, and the crowd
seemed most interested in what she had to say.

After the conference, Rich asked to see the results of
the kids' evaluations of the event. He saw the scores that

he and the other speakers received. They were good numbers, but he wondered how the kids scored the girl who spoke. He feared she'd be humiliated. But her presentation ranked the highest of all!

And that brings us to a set of guidelines when asking young people to evaluate their youth ministries:

1. Don't make assumptions. As the above story illustrates, young people's opinions often surprise us. After working with a group of young people for several years, we may get a feel for their opinions. But we will never know them completely unless we ask. If we are to remain effective, we must continually seek kids' feedback.

2. Poll every young person, not just a select few. We know a youth pastor who bases big decisions on the opinions of a couple of kids. He'll schedule a big trip, then later have to cancel it for lack of interest. Obviously the two kids who told him the trip would be great didn't represent a significant portion of the group.

3. Query the inactives too. Often it's the kids who rarely show up who really need the ministry. Be sure to include them when evaluating. Give them questionnaires to fill out. It's best to have them fill out the questionnaire on the spot. Otherwise, you probably will not see the questionnaire again. The most effective process is to bring questionnaires to the inactives in their homes, have them fill them out while you wait, and then to talk with them briefly before leaving.

4. Encourage candid evaluations. Make it comfortable for kids to be honest. Don't ask for a show of hands to the question, "How many of you think I talk too much?" Use the anonymous questionnaire method when seeking potentially sensitive information. Let kids know that you value their *honest* feelings. Set an atmosphere of openness. Don't attempt to manipulate the kids' responses. And never pooh-pooh their opinions or dismiss their

responses with excuses.

Evaluation by your young people is a crucial first step toward implementing youth-based ministry. If this approach is to succeed in your church, you'll need to begin with solid information. We'll supply you with several evaluation tools to get you started.

Evaluation Tool 1: The Sack Poll. Here's an evaluation model we've used successfully with our kids. Get a bunch of small (lunch-bag size) paper sacks. Write on each bag a possible quality or statement about your youth ministry. Some examples:

"My opinion counts here."
"I feel comfortable bringing my friends."
"This group is run by adults."
"I feel welcome in this group."
"I feel needed by this group."
"This congregation cares about teenagers."
"If our leader were to leave, this group would fall apart."
"This group cares about me."
"I've felt closer to God through this group."
"This group deals with issues that are important to me."
"We need more adults at activities."
"Bible studies."
"Retreats."
"Lock-ins."
"Youth choir."
"Weekly meetings."
"Trips."
"Singing."
"Prayer."
"Worship."
"Discussions."
"Games."

Issues that are imp to me..

Others

"Service projects."

"The leader's talks."

Now tape or tack the sacks, open side up, to a wall. Give each kid a stack of green and a stack of red slips of paper. (These can be cut to about 1"×3" from construction paper.) Red and green index cards can also be used. Ask the young people to wander past the row of sacks on the wall. If they agree with a statement on a sack, they should drop in a green slip. If they disagree, they should deposit a red slip. In sacks labeled with activities such as "Bible studies" and "Retreats," kids should deposit green slips if they feel these functions have been helpful to them; red slips if they feel the activities have not been helpful.

Now divide the bags among your kids. Let them tally the votes and mark the results on the outside of the sacks. Then, in groups no larger than eight, discuss the results. Why did certain bags get mostly green slips? Why did some fill with red slips?

Or, ask kids to write their opinions why some bags were filled predominately with red slips and have them drop their opinions back in the sacks. This is helpful, particularly with sensitive issues.

You'll find this experiential survey a fun way to uncover some real feelings among your active members. And you'll be able to see how youth-based ministry might affect your kids.

Now, ideas for helping inactives evaluate the youth ministry:

Evaluation Tool 2: A Questionnaire for Inactive Youth. As we mentioned before, your inactive young people are prime targets to poll. Chart 1 is a sample questionnaire that will help to reveal some of their important feelings. You will, of course, want to adapt it to your own unique situation. Again, it is best to take questionnaires to inactives and have them fill them out while you wait. But if you mail questionnaires to inactives, always include a self-addressed stamped envelope; otherwise you will receive few completed questionnaires.

CHART 1

Confidential Questionnaire About
First Church's Youth Ministry

Your opinion is important to us. Please take a moment to complete this confidential survey. Your answers will be combined with others to help us design a better youth ministry at First Church. When you're finished, just put this questionnaire into the enclosed self-addressed stamped envelope and drop it in the mail. Your opinions will be kept strictly confidential. Thanks!

1. When I hear about church activities, I may **not** attend because (check all that apply):

_____ a. I don't know anyone in the group.

_____ b. I don't like the people in the group.

_____ c. I think it will be boring.

_____ d. It won't be fun.

_____ e. I have to work.

_____ f. It's too religious.

_____ g. It's too much "fun and games."

_____ h. I don't like the adult leaders.

_____ i. I have too much homework.

_____ j. Other: _____.

2. What are your feelings about the youth group at First Church? Show your agreement or disagreement with the following statements by circling a number.

	Strongly agree										Strongly disagree
a. The youth group needs me.	10	9	8	7	6	5	4	3	2	1	0

b. The youth group is run
   by one adult.   10 9 8 7 6 5 4 3 2 1 0

c. The youth group is run
   by a few kids.   10 9 8 7 6 5 4 3 2 1 0

d. The youth group
   welcomes newcomers.   10 9 8 7 6 5 4 3 2 1 0

e. The youth group is
   friendly.   10 9 8 7 6 5 4 3 2 1 0

f. The youth group deals
   with issues that are
   important to me.   10 9 8 7 6 5 4 3 2 1 0

3. How would you grade the following youth group activities at First Church? (Circle one grade per item.)

	A	B	C	D	F
a. Bible studies	A	B	C	D	F
b. Retreats	A	B	C	D	F
c. Lock-ins	A	B	C	D	F
d. Youth choir	A	B	C	D	F
e. Weekly meetings	A	B	C	D	F
f. Trips	A	B	C	D	F
g. Singing	A	B	C	D	F
h. Prayer	A	B	C	D	F
i. Worship	A	B	C	D	F
j. Discussions	A	B	C	D	F
k. Games	A	B	C	D	F
l. Pastor's talks	A	B	C	D	F
m. Service projects	A	B	C	D	F

The results of this survey should give you many ideas for new directions for your youth ministry. Look carefully at the results under Question 2. If you see some discouraging scores here, youth-based ministry could have a dramatic effect on attracting your inactives back to the group.

Most likely, your inactives choose not to attend because their needs aren't being met. And, most likely, those needs include the basics of self-esteem, self-confidence and the need to be needed.

Youth-based ministry addresses these needs in a powerful, experiential way. Our youth group experienced much growth in attendance after the implementation of youth-based ministry. Almost all of that growth came from the inactive roster. The new approach obviously met real needs.

Evaluation by the Parents

More and more, we are coming to realize that good youth ministry means family ministry. But for years, many youth workers took an almost anti-family approach. "Hey, look how these parents have fouled up their kids," they'd say. "Now we have to straighten out 15 years of damage done by the parents." Youth workers saw themselves as counterforces to families.

Today, aware youth workers admit that their influence over an adolescent pales compared to the parents'. If we are to maximize our ministry potential, we must find ways to help parents do their adolescent rearing.

Most parents truly love their teenage kids. They're interested in their sons' and daughters' activities. The more information that parents receive about their church's youth ministry, the more support they're likely to give.

Complaining parents make any youth worker's job frustrating. But we've found a direct link between parental gripes and the amount of youth ministry information (or lack thereof) they receive. The rule of "the fewer the surprises, the fewer the complaints" is very true in youth work.

Youth-based ministry needs good parental support. Begin by involving them in the evaluation process. Warning: This can be painful (and sometimes confusing). So often we've seen two sets of parents make directly opposite evaluations of a youth ministry. One will say, "Your youth ministry isn't spiritual enough. It's nothing but a bunch of parties." And another will describe the same youth ministry as "too religious." But parental input is vital. When we go to the trouble of asking their opinions, they feel involved, invested.

Chart 2 is a sample questionnaire to be used with parents before launching into a new youth-based ministry. Ask them to complete the questionnaire at a special parents meeting, or before or after church services, or through the mail. Don't forget to include parents of inactive youth. You'll want to adapt the questionnaire to fit your unique situation.

CHART 2
Confidential Questionnaire for
Parents of High School Youth

Please help us make the youth ministry at First Church the best it can be. We want to serve you and your young people. Please take a moment to complete this brief questionnaire and return it to the youth ministry office by next Sunday. Your responses will be kept in strict confidentiality.

Circle the number at right that best describes your opinion.

	Strongly agree	Strongly disagree
1. The youth ministry at First Church helps my child feel loved.	10 9 8 7 6 5 4 3 2 1 0	
2. The youth ministry makes my child feel needed.	10 9 8 7 6 5 4 3 2 1 0	

3. The youth ministry meets
   my child's needs.   10 9 8 7 6 5 4 3 2 1 0

4. The youth ministry uses my
   child's talents and abilities.   10 9 8 7 6 5 4 3 2 1 0

5. The youth ministry helps my
   child's faith grow.   10 9 8 7 6 5 4 3 2 1 0

6. The youth ministry seems to
   be for a select few.   10 9 8 7 6 5 4 3 2 1 0

7. Youth ministry leaders inform
   me about what's going on.   10 9 8 7 6 5 4 3 2 1 0

8. The youth ministry enhances
   our family relationships.   10 9 8 7 6 5 4 3 2 1 0

9. The youth ministry asks too
   much of parents.   10 9 8 7 6 5 4 3 2 1 0

Please give each of the following elements of our youth ministry a grade, according to how effective you perceive it to be. (Circle one letter grade for each item.)

	A	B	C	D	F
a. Spiritual emphasis	A	B	C	D	F
b. Building friendships	A	B	C	D	F
c. Having fun/social time	A	B	C	D	F
d. Service projects	A	B	C	D	F
e. Learning Christian values	A	B	C	D	F
f. Outreach to non-churched young people	A	B	C	D	F

Evaluation by Volunteer Adult Youth Workers

Volunteers are key people in most successful youth ministries. But often their needs have never been examined. Chart 3 is a survey that will help you inventory some of these needs. You may discover what motivates your adults to help in the youth ministry department. You also may discover why some adults might feel uncomfortable with youth-based ministry.

Ask all of your adult volunteers—and others who you believe might make good volunteers in youth-based ministry—to fill out the survey. You should also take this survey yourself. Try it right now! It is *essential* that you yourself answer these questions before reading further.

CHART 3
Youth Ministry Survey

Name _____

Please help us make the youth ministry at First Church more effective. Take a moment to complete this brief questionnaire. It will help us get to know you better. For each of the following questions, you may check one answer. Now, we know that with several of the questions, you'll feel like checking more than one answer. But you need to check the *one* answer that you feel strongest about. There are no "right" or "wrong" answers to these questions, so respond with your real feelings. Have fun!

1. When kids arrive for youth group activities, I usually: (Check one only.)
_____ a. try to get everyone and everything organized.
_____ b. enjoy spending time with kids I've been building good relationships with.
_____ c. help newcomers and loner-types blend into the group.
_____ d. sit and wait for things to begin.

2. During youth group games or funny skits, I like to: (Check one only.)
_____ a. give the instructions and direct the activities.
_____ b. give the kids a good laugh with my sense of humor.
_____ c. participate along with the kids in the games.
_____ d. stand aside and observe.

3. The kids in our group learn best when I: (Check one only.)

_____ a. prepare a lesson and give a talk.

_____ b. talk one-on-one with kids who've grown to be my friends.

_____ c. participate along with the kids in a group discussion.

_____ d. remain quiet and let them make their own discoveries.

4. An adult who works with kids in our church should: (Check one only.)

_____ a. be a guide and adviser.

_____ b. be the kids' close friend—at church and socially.

_____ c. be a partner with the kids in growth and learning.

_____ d. let the kids lead—it's their group.

5. TASK   PEOPLE

_____

If the above continuum represents my approach to youth ministry leadership, the kids would probably place me: (Check one only.)

_____ a. toward the task end. I like to make sure all the details are covered and everything is prepared for each activity so that the kids have a good experience.

_____ b. toward the people end. I like to spend most of my time building quality relationships with the kids.

_____ c. in the middle. I like to divide my time between making program preparations and spending time with the group.

_____ d. toward the people end. I enjoy being around when the kids are involved in various activities.

6. If I caught one of our kids drinking beer at a retreat, I would probably: (Check one only.)

_____ a. send the kid home because he broke the rules.

_____ b. not send him home. I'd talk with him about the problem, in hopes of keeping our relationship intact.

_____ c. talk with him and with the group and decide what action should be taken.

_____ d. say nothing to the kid and keep the matter quiet.

7. If one of our young people came to me with a deep problem, even if she was contemplating suicide, I'd probably: (Check one only.)

_____ a. give the young person the necessary direction for overcoming her problems.

_____ b. feel honored that she shared this with me. And I'd assure her that I would maintain confidentiality.

_____ c. listen carefully, then help the young person make arrangements for professional help.

_____ d. pray for her and ask her to seek God's guidance.

8. The strength of any good youth ministry is based on: (Check one only.)

_____ a. the leadership, gifts and abilities of concerned adults.

_____ b. the relationships that adult leaders build with kids.

_____ c. the involvement and commitment of youth and adults.

_____ d. the kids taking their responsibilities seriously.

9. My favorite aspect of my involvement with our youth ministry is: (Check one only.)

_____ a. speaking or leading songs for the group.

_____ b. goofing around with the kids.

_____ c. watching and helping kids grow and assume more leadership.

_____ d. the fellowship with the other adults.

10. In our youth ministry, non-Christian kids would most likely come to the faith through: (Check one only.)

_____ a. our leader's preaching or teaching.

_____ b. a one-on-one relationship with one of our adults.

_____ c. a one-on-one relationship with one of our young people.

_____ d. reading the Bible.

After finishing the questionnaire, add up the number of "A" responses you checked. Also total your "B," "C" and "D" responses. Do the same for each of your adult volunteers.

Study the totals, not the individual questions. The "best" answer for an individual may be highly debatable. For some questions, all four responses would make good answers. What you're looking for here is a trend that might indicate a person's leadership style.

The "A" types. Adults who chose predominately "A" responses may lean toward an authoritarian leadership style. They may tend to approach youth ministry from a military model. That is, they may see themselves and other adults as the order-givers, and the kids as subservient followers. These adults may also crave the attention and power that an up-front leader might command.

These "A-style" leaders may find youth-based ministry unusually discomforting. They may initially resist its implementation and later may grumble at the kids' attempts at leadership. They can be won over to youth-based ministry, but probably will need ongoing reminders about its goals and techniques. Make a special effort to point out to them the growth among your young people as it occurs during youth-based ministry.

Some "A" types can be used successfully on special committees and task forces. However, some "A" types may be too dictatorial and shouldn't be considered in a youth-based ministry program.

The "B" types. People whose responses are weighted with "B" answers may be "social creatures." Typically extroverts, they love relating to the kids on a personal level. They often need the kids' friendship. Look carefully to see if these adults have solid relationships with people their own age. If they do not, they may be using the youth group to satisfy their own needs for intimacy. This may cause them to make unhealthy decisions such as placing higher priority on their relationships than on the ultimate welfare of the kids. Young people don't need an adult "buddy" who acts like the rest of the adolescent gang. They need significant adults who act like adults—to model good Christian adult behavior and values. And many healthy "B" people do a fine job of this.

Healthy "B" types generally adapt fairly well to youth-based ministry. However, they do require special handling. Their belief system tells them that the kids' growth depends upon relationships with "big brother" or "big sister" adult leaders. It may never occur to them that young people are capable of ministering to one another. Monitor these adults. Counsel them if they appear to dominate discussion times. Match their "big brother" or "big sister" skills with young people who really need that type of interaction such as kids from single-parent homes.

The "C" types. Adults with many "C" responses tend to believe in young people. They typically design their adult involvement around what will help elevate the kids to greater levels of involvement and Christian growth. They may be gifted with the finesse of knowing just how much to say and do to help young people believe they made big strides and accomplishments all on their own.

"C" people usually don't involve themselves in youth ministry to draw attention to themselves. They are naturals for youth-based ministry.

The "D" types. At first glance, "D" people look like quintessential youth-based ministry types. "Let the kids do their thing," they may say. But don't be fooled. These adults do not understand youth-based ministry.

These are the "stand-back-and-let-the-kids-fall-flat-on-their-faces" people. They typically display a detached attitude. They may be more interested in spectating than serving. "D" types may become highly frustrated when kids neglect a responsibility in youth-based ministry.

When asked to help remind kids of their duties, "D" adults may say, "What for? Those kids are old enough to do that without my reminder. They need to learn to be responsible." Most "D" types should be encouraged to serve the church somewhere outside of youth ministry. The veneer of their philosophy appears to be youth-based. But they're dangerous to a ministry that seeks to do the hard adult work of building a subtle framework that helps kids succeed and grow.

Evaluation by the Church Staff

Youth ministry shouldn't be isolated from the rest of the church. Truly effective youth ministries connect throughout all aspects of church life. Church people who understand this don't say, "Young people are the church of tomorrow." They say, "Young people are the church of today." They remember young people when planning everything from sermons to potluck suppers to Christian education opportunities to new building plans to evangelism outreach to missions programs.

Young people benefit from their inclusion in the total life of the church. And the church benefits too. The inclusion of youth demonstrates that the church is one of society's few genuinely intergenerational institutions. The Christian walk spans a lifetime.

Connection with the rest of church life is a significant advantage that church youth ministry has over parachurch youth ministry. Organizations such as Young Life, Youth for Christ and Campus Crusade for Christ do some good work in the area of evangelism. But what happens to the kids after a couple of years, when they grow out of these clubs? There's no place for them to go.

The church provides for a young Christian's ongoing faith journey. We need to do what we can to reinforce this golden connection. And youth ministry people can begin that process by seeking the input of the whole church staff.

Chart 4 is a sample questionnaire to give to your church staff. Ask all of your staff people to complete one. Don't forget to include the custodian and church secretary. These key people often wield the subtle power to make or break a youth ministry. Your interest in their input can make a real difference.

CHART 4
Youth Ministry Questionnaire for Church Staff

The success of the youth ministry depends on all of us here at First Church. As staff people, your opinions and ideas are valuable and vital. Please help us shape the future of youth ministry by completing this brief questionnaire.

1. Why should a youth ministry exist at our church? (Check all that apply. Then rank your choices, marking the most compelling reason with a "1," the next with a "2," and so on.)

_____ for the evangelism of youth

_____ to deepen kids' faith

_____ to meet kids' various needs

_____ to help kids grow

_____ to attract whole families into the congregation through youth visibility

_____ to involve kids in the life of the church

_____ to teach healthy values to kids

_____ to provide an avenue for kids to express their gifts

_____ to give kids a chance to serve

_____ Other: _____

2. My role in youth ministry, as a member of our church staff, is:
(Check any that apply.)

_____ to give support.

_____ to be an advocate for youth.

_____ to communicate with youth.

_____ to be a resource person.

_____ to give prayer support.

_____ to give of my time.

_____ to give financial support.

_____ Other: _____

3. A thriving youth ministry will help our congregation because:

_____

_____

_____

_____

_____

_____

_____

After administering this questionnaire to your staff,
compare and contrast the results. Discuss the meaning of
similar and differing answers among the staff. Even the
survey questions themselves often open eyes to the vital
role youth ministry plays in the life of a congregation.

As you consider youth-based ministry, set the precedent for staff involvement *now*. Without good staff
support, youth-based ministry faces two dangerous possibilities: misinterpreted failure and envious success.

Failure. If not carefully educated and re-educated,
senior ministers and other church staff members often

misinterpret a youth-based group's temporary failures as catastrophic, personally embarrassing and evidence of the youth minister's ineptitude.

Success. We've seen a number of youth ministries that have failed because they were too successful. Problems arose when the youth ministry became highly visible in the congregation and community. People all over town talked about these successful youth programs. But the youth ministry leadership failed to keep top church leadership informed. Some of the "old guard" young people and adults resented the change that growth brought. So, senior ministers and other leaders began to resent the youth ministry's cavalier operation. Since the church leaders felt detached from the youth ministry, they perceived its success as something that made them and their own programs look bad by comparison.

Communication with and evaluation by staff and congregational leadership is essential to any healthy youth ministry.

Evaluation by You

Since you're reading this book, you're probably in a position to influence the structure of your church's youth ministry. If you're that important, it's necessary to take a good look at yourself and your own abilities. Your influence on youth ministry in the past may be due to your own beliefs and background. It may intrigue you to explore your belief system to see its impact on your church's youth ministry.

Chart 5 is for you alone. Dive into this personal evaluation. Be honest. Take it seriously. And see what you can discover.

CHART 5
My Evaluation of Our Church's Youth Ministry Right Now

A. My perception of youth ministry ownership

Our church's youth ministry is *best* described as . . . (check one)

_____ *my* youth ministry.

_____ *their* youth ministry.

_____ *our* youth ministry.

Give three reasons why you feel that way:

1. _____.

2. _____.

3. _____.

If your answers reflect a "me, mine, I" or "their, them, they" flavor, your youth ministry could be struggling with an ownership problem. Words such as "ours, we, us" portray a "we're-in-this-together" attitude. Youth-based ministry can promote that togetherness approach.

B. My perception of youth ministry responsibility

Circle the response you feel best reflects your church's youth ministry:

1. Kids follow through with their responsibility. always/sometimes/never

2. Adults follow through with their responsibility. always/sometimes/never

3. Group members take a great deal of ownership in the youth ministry. always/sometimes/never

4. Kids are involved in planning our programs and activities. always/sometimes/never

5. Kids are involved in leading
our programs and activities.   always/sometimes/never

6. Young people provide high
visibility for the church's
youth ministry.   always/sometimes/never

7. The congregation views
young people as valuable
members of the church.   always/sometimes/never

8. The same people do all the
work in our youth ministry.   always/sometimes/never

9. Our programs offer young
people an opportunity to
grow in responsibility and
leadership.   always/sometimes/never

Answering "always" or "sometimes" for all the statements except 8 shows you're already involved in youth-based ministry to some degree. When youth-based ministry begins to fly, statement 8 changes from the "same people doing all the work" to "a variety of kids and adults making ministry happen."

C. My perception of our youth ministry structure

Circle which diagram best represents your youth group's leadership structure right now:

1. Military model   **2. Representative model**   **3. Group process model**

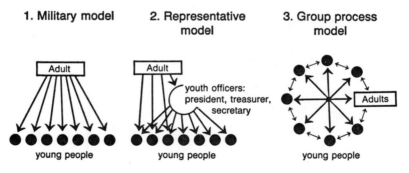

(For a more detailed explanation of each model, see page 55.)

If you did not circle "group process model," what impact would a change to this model have on your present ministry?

If you did circle "group process model," what are your frustrations with the model? your joys?

Youth ministry can happen under each structure pictured above. But the benefits of youth-based ministry occur when a group practices the group process. Both the military model and representative model have their place under certain circumstances. But for the greatest growth, ownership and shared-leadership responsibility, the intricate web work of group interaction works best.

You'll need to take a close look at the other models and see where you currently feel most comfortable. Or, to see where you'll need to grow.

The following evaluations will help you do that.

D. My perception of the purpose of our youth ministry

Youth ministry exists in our church for the purpose of: (Check all that apply.)

_____ evangelizing young people.

_____ deepening kids' faith.

_____ meeting kids' various needs.

_____ helping kids grow.

_____ attracting whole families into the congregation through high youth visibility.

_____ involving kids in the life of the church.

_____ teaching healthy values to teenagers.

_____ providing an avenue for kids to express their gifts.

_____ giving kids a chance to serve.

_____ other: _____

Our present organizational structure is in place because it: (Check all that apply.)

_____ accomplishes the above goals.

_____ benefits the young people.

_____ makes my job easier.

_____ has always been done that way.

_____ has never been thought about in any other way.

_____ provides visibility for young people.

_____ provides visibility for me.

_____ pleases the "powers that be."

_____ other: _____

Youth-based ministry strives to meet the needs and to fulfill the purpose of the group through its structured framework. Does your present organizational structure help accomplish the youth ministry's goals and benefit young people? If you're uncertain, it might be time for a youth ministry make over.

E. My connection and contribution to our youth ministry right now

Place an "X" on each line in the "Me-O-Meter" showing what best describes your leadership style right now.

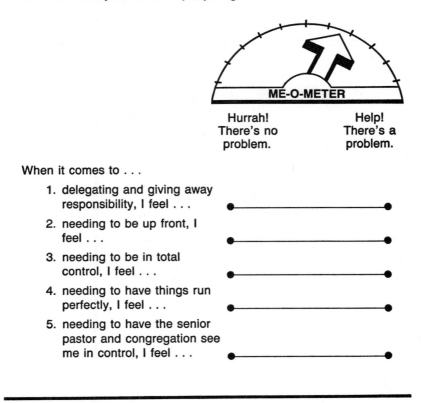

ME-O-METER

| Hurrah! There's no problem. | Help! There's a problem. |

When it comes to . . .

1. delegating and giving away responsibility, I feel . . .

2. needing to be up front, I feel . . .

3. needing to be in total control, I feel . . .

4. needing to have things run perfectly, I feel . . .

5. needing to have the senior pastor and congregation see me in control, I feel . . .

Being able to lead and implement youth-based ministry requires a certain comfort with giving leadership away without abandoning kids. If the "Me-O-Meter" reflects a pattern of "Hurrahs," you should find this form of leadership a natural. If the meter shows a few "Helps," you might feel a few personal pinches and pulls when it comes to enforcing a youth-based ministry leadership style.

If you haven't completed the "Youth Ministry Survey" on page 41, do so now. Total your score. What did you discover?

If you see lots of "C" answers, you'll find it easy to adapt to the youth-based ministry style. If your answers fall into the other categories, it doesn't mean youth-based ministry isn't for you; it means you'll probably have to work harder at it. Plan to surround yourself with plenty of "C" types for support, encouragement and hope.

You can do it! The fun of this style of ministry is that everybody grows. Adults and kids alike. All group members are encouraged to become all they can be as God's children—adult leaders included!

Evaluation of Various Youth Ministry Structures

So, is youth-based ministry right for your situation? Take a look at the comparisons of youth ministry structures in Chart 6. At a glance, you'll see some advantages and disadvantages to three different forms of youth ministry organization.

CHART 6
Three Youth Ministry Models

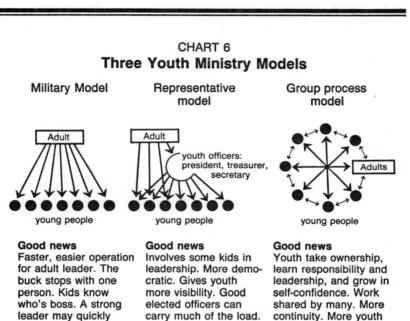

Military Model	Representative model	Group process model

Good news

Faster, easier operation for adult leader. The buck stops with one person. Kids know who's boss. A strong leader may quickly attract new members. Easy for kids to drop in and out of group without worry of responsibility. Works well for businesses and military.

Bad news

The whole ministry depends on the strengths (and weaknesses) of one or more adult leaders. When strong leader leaves, youth ministry frequently collapses. Kids are denied the opportunity to learn responsibility, leadership, organization. No youth ownership. Adult(s) often does all the legwork.

Good news

Involves some kids in leadership. More democratic. Gives youth more visibility. Good elected officers can carry much of the load. Lets kids sample the representative form of government. Works well for national and state governments.

Bad news

Youth officers may be elected by popularity. Those not elected may have hard feelings. Only a few kids given a chance to lead. May burn out officers. Adult often does everything anyway, making youth officers simply figureheads. Little or no youth ownership. Occasional confusion about who's really in charge.

Good news

Youth take ownership, learn responsibility and leadership, and grow in self-confidence. Work shared by many. More continuity. More youth visibility. Full youth involvement possible. Works well in friendships and in youth ministry.

Bad news

Often a greater chance for failure of some activities and programs. Adults may get congregation's blame for failures. May be slower, more cumbersome. Requires new skills from adults. "Star-oriented" youth workers may feel frustrated.

We trust that the evaluation tools in this chapter have helped you to gain a more accurate view of your present ministry and a clearer vision for new opportunities in youth ministry. By now you should be convinced that youth-based ministry is *not* the easy way out. Of all the possible youth ministry structures, youth-based ministry requires the most finesse and skill from the adult leaders. But, happily, this skill is learnable. And the benefits of youth-based ministry should provide for more long-term stability and growth. That means that even if you're not the funniest, best looking, most articulate, most musical youth worker in town, you can still provide the most effective youth ministry. In the next chapter, let's look at how to move toward youth-based ministry.

CHAPTER FOUR

Moving Toward Youth-Based Ministry

So, you've decided that youth-based ministry is right for you and your church. What's next? Do you jump right in? Or, do you phase this new structure into your ministry over several months? What about the people currently holding youth ministry leadership positions? These are important questions.

Most of us find change uncomfortable. We all love the security of familiarity. When we're faced with different ways of doing things, we usually resist. That makes it necessary for change agents to plan their strategy carefully to ensure they make progress without creating undue discomfort. The "burden of proof" is on the shoulders of those who lobby for change. In a very real sense, you must "sell" the idea of youth-based ministry—young people and adults will ultimately decide whether the benefits of change outweigh the perceived loss of current benefits or specter of new problems.

Explaining the Dream

First, talk with your key people about youth-based ministry. Meet informally and individually with each adult working with the youth ministry. Do the same with church staff members, congregational leaders and key young people.

Offer your reflections of the evaluations you've tabulated. Point out areas where the youth ministry can grow. Then explain youth-based ministry. Review the benefits noted in Chapter 2. Also, candidly discuss the dangers and risks of youth-based ministry. Answer their questions and listen to their concerns and ideas.

Do you sense some interest in pursuing youth-based ministry? If so, gather interested people to dream of such a ministry's possibilities. Once again, discuss the results of the evaluations and explain the pros and cons of youth-based ministry. Seek a consensus for presenting the concept to the youth group.

At a special or regular youth group meeting, explain youth-based ministry to your young people. Fully explain the benefits and dangers. You may wish to present the change as a trial arrangement—for a period of one year, for example. Ask the young people to vote (using secret ballots) on whether to proceed with youth-based ministry.

Timing Your Move

When should the switch to youth-based ministry be made? That decision depends upon your situation and preferences.

You may choose a natural transition point such as the

beginning of the school year, the beginning of summer, the start of a new calendar year, or at the end of current officers' terms. Most of us already are conditioned to these times as points for change or for fresh starts.

Or, you may prefer to initiate youth-based ministry at an inconspicuous time—maybe in November or March. This timing may draw more attention to the switch, because changes aren't expected at this time of year.

Most important, make the switch only after you've carefully prepared. Take all the time necessary to thoroughly evaluate, talk to key people, meet with your young people, recruit qualified adults, and plan for an effective kick-off event and other programming. Do not attempt to launch youth-based ministry if you and your team cannot invest the up-front time required for planning.

Letting Your Group Die

The success of youth-based ministry is greatly enhanced if attention is drawn to its inception. Don't try to sneak it into being. Celebrate its newness!

We've found it most successful to make a clean break from the old youth ministry structure. Phasing in elements of youth-based ministry dilutes its effectiveness. In order to work, this structure needs to be implemented all at once. There are too many interrelated components to expect success by simply hooking up a couple of features.

Before severing your current structure, be sensitive to its present leaders—adults and youth. If not handled carefully, feelings can be irreversibly wounded. Kathy was the president of our youth group. Becoming president was a big deal for Kathy. She basked in her title. When the group elected to try youth-based ministry, Kathy didn't hide her lack of enthusiasm. But the group asked her to serve on the planning task force for the new structure.

She came to the first two planning meetings, then withdrew completely. Her need for presidential recognition overrode her commitment to the group. We tried talking with her about her feelings, but she wouldn't open up. The damage had been done. We now know that we should have spent more time with her, individually, in the early stages of our exploration into youth-based ministry. And we should have done more to affirm her for her contribution to the old group. We didn't provide proper closure of the old group.

Before youth-based ministry is initiated, the old structure should be carefully and respectfully laid to rest. It needs to die in order for new life to emerge. We think of resurrection stories and Jesus' words: "A grain of wheat remains no more than a single grain unless it is dropped into the ground and dies. If it does die, then it produces many grains" (John 12:24).

The old group must die so that the new group may live. But before you say goodbye to the old, pause to celebrate the many good memories. Plan a special get-together to reminisce. Everyone needs to know that the old is finished and the new is about to begin!

Burying Your Old Group

Your old group deserves a decent burial. Plan a funeral! At a special meeting, spend some time remembering "the good old days." Retell the stories of that canoe trip in the rain. And that retreat where John and Andy were sent home for filling the Reverend Troutman's underwear with itching powder.

Maybe you'll create a treasure chest or scrapbook of the old group—even add an epitaph, for how the group wants to be remembered.

Let kids mourn. Give them permission to talk and cry

about the old group. Don't rob them of the natural sense of loss which occurs in any change.

Perhaps you'll want to share and write down the things group members want to "get rid of"; then actually burn, destroy or bury the list.

Then mention that the group has shared many good—and bad—times together. But now it's time to lay this group to rest so that another may come to life. Reach for your church's official committal service and begin reading. It may go something like this:

"We are gathered here today to commit the Youth Fellowship of First Church to the earth—dust to dust and ashes to ashes in the sure and certain hope of the resurrection."

Then sing a song such as "I Am the Resurrection."

Join in prayer and depart with the reminder that your next meeting will mark the beginning of new life!

This ceremony often has a stunning effect on young people.

Quieting Talk About the Old Group

Years ago, the youth ministry at our church enjoyed a couple of years of high visibility. But the kids in that group graduated and went off to college. A few years of remission followed. Then, the leadership decided to investigate youth-based ministry. But every time some-one mentioned the youth ministry's future and potential, somebody else would refer fondly to the youth group of long ago. Parents, adult volunteers, church council members and younger siblings of past group members would say, "Why can't the group be like it used to?" or, "You won't be able to make the group as good as it was back then."

All that talk was not only demoralizing, it was skewed.

The old group was not a perfect example of youth ministry. But, as often happens, the passing years tended to sugarcoat many people's memories.

This is a particularly common phenomenon facing a new youth minister who follows a recently departed, well-liked leader. The memories of the glorious times of the past take on a life of their own, growing to statuesque proportions. Nostalgia is a common defense against dealing with the here-and-now situation.

Constant comparisons to the old group, the old leader or the old way of doing things serve no positive purpose. When stepping out into youth-based ministry, put a moratorium on talk about the old group. Make direct (and positive) requests to the kids, adults, parents and church leaders. You might say, "I know that many of you have good memories of the old group. I've heard many references to the way things were. It's fun to remember. But now is a time of new beginnings for our youth ministry. We're trying to be as careful as we can to build the most effective ministry possible. But as we're planning and launching into fresh starts, it is discouraging to hear comparisons to the 'good old days.' Will you help us build the youth ministry into everything it can be? You can help by agreeing to set aside all references to the old group for the next few months."

This approach worked marvelously well at our church. People seemed to appreciate and respect our directness. And, with the fable-casters silenced, we were able to proceed more efficiently.

Shutting Down the Youth Group

What happens to the current youth group while a new ministry is being designed? It can continue in its traditional mode. Or, you may wish to consider the radical choice of shutting it down for a time.

At our church, the young people and adult leaders agreed to cease all youth group meetings and activities while we worked on the new youth-based structure. So, for four months the church calendar showed no regular youth programs. Special activities continued, however.

During the shutdown, curiosity in the "new, improved" youth ministry began to mushroom. "What are you guys planning?" the kids asked. Parents became a little edgy, wondering when weekly meetings for their kids would begin again.

Temporarily "boarding up" the youth group worked well for us. It helped us make a clean break from the old youth ministry, a break which we perceived as necessary.

A temporary shutdown offers several advantages:

► Shutting down grabs attention and builds curiosity. Your chances for success with youth-based ministry are enhanced if everyone sees it as a really different approach. Placing a time gap between the old and the new helps signal the switch.

► Shutting down allows quality time to plan for the start-up of youth-based ministry. You'll probably want to meet at least weekly with your planning task force, which should include your key young people. Their busy schedules may demand limiting their weekly commitments in order to devote the necessary time to building the foundation for youth-based ministry.

► Shutting down builds anticipation. During the shutdown period, young people may yearn to get together regularly again with their friends from church. Greater interest and increased attendance may result at your kickoff event for youth-based ministry.

A shutdown could span a few weeks or a few months. Keep communicating with the kids, parents and church leaders during this time. Remind everyone that the youth ministry hasn't disappeared forever; it is, in fact, working very hard to build something new and more effective. You may wish to "leak" a few of your plans to the congregation via the "press"—your church newsletters and worship bulletins.

Utilizing an Administrative Team

A responsible church body should oversee the planning and continuous operation of any youth ministry. This applies to youth-based ministry too. This administrative team may advise and guide the youth-based ministry planning task force as it builds new ministry foundations.

You may already have this team in place in the form of a youth board that's comprised of interested adults who are elected by the congregation. If not, you will need to form an administrative team.

This team of adults is a key element in the intricate structure of youth-based ministry. The administrative team lends perspective and helps to interpret youth-based ministry to church leaders and to the congregation on a continuing basis.

See the next chapter for more details on the administrative team.

Setting Up a Planning Task Force

Now you're ready to work out all the details for your new youth-based ministry. Form a team of youth and adults who'll do the planning for your conversion to this new approach. These people will have the big job of building the framework that others later will use to make this ministry work. Chapter 6 will lead you through the planning task force's composition and duties.

CHAPTER FIVE

The Administrative Team

A t first glance, some people assume youth-based ministry is just a bunch of kids doing whatever they want. That's not the case. This organizational structure needs links of accountability to function with any continuity.

Youth-based ministry begins at an "executive" level with the administrative team. This small group of adults oversees the youth ministry to assure that overall ministry goals are being met. Under the administrative team are the temporary planning task force and the ongoing steering committee, both of which are primarily composed of youth. These youth-based bodies plan the direction of the youth group. Chart 7 illustrates the paths of accountability for youth-based ministry.

CHART 7
Youth-Based Ministry Organizational Structure

Administrative Team
(quality control, recruiters of volunteer adults, resource
providers, trainers, link to the congregation)

Temporary Planning Task Force
(writers of the "constitution" for the new youth ministry)
and
Steering Committee
(ongoing planners of programming, policy-makers)

Youth Group
(decision-makers, doers)

An administrative team may already exist at your church. You might be calling it the "youth board," "youth council" or "youth ministry committee." Whatever it's called, it usually consists of adults, elected or selected, who have an interest in youth ministry. This body often oversees and supports youth ministry personnel, whether they're paid staffers or volunteers.

If your church does not have such an official board or committee, you will need to form one to aid in the administration of youth-based ministry. The administrative team need not be large. Three or four is fine. It may be comprised of the pastor or youth minister plus two or three adult volunteers who've had experience with young people. Perhaps they've previously served as sponsors.

Or, you may wish to include experienced school teachers on this team.

We do not recommend including young people on this team. The administrative team's responsibilities include personnel issues—"hiring and firing" of adult volunteers, etc. Highly sensitive information about volunteers is often discussed. Though young people's input may be important on issues such as these, the kids shouldn't be asked to assume the burden of adjudicating such delicate matters. Besides, the kids' energies and creativity are best used at the planning and action levels, rather than on the administrative level.

It's important that the administrative team thoroughly understands and supports youth-based ministry. These people will be your objective observers for this new form of youth ministry.

The Administrative Team's Role

The administrative team performs several vital functions to ensure the ongoing success of youth-based ministry. But the team's work is primarily "behind the scenes." The young people may never know about much of the work of the administrative team. And that's okay.

Here's a look at the administrative team's duties:

1. Supervising. The administrative team serves as a guide and as a quality control for the planning task force, steering committee and youth group. The administrative team should stay in close touch with the primary person responsible for youth ministry in the congregation. This person may be a paid staff member—youth minister, associate or senior pastor, or director of Christian education. Sometimes the primary person is an adult volunteer. The administrative team assists the adult youth workers by keeping the goals and practices of youth-based ministry in focus.

2. Providing resources. The adults in youth-based
ministry carry the important responsibility of supplying
teenage decision-makers with options and resources. The
administrative team can serve the adult youth workers by
furnishing them with good resources and ideas. These
resources might include books, magazines, curricula and
people.

3. Recruiting adult volunteers. Not everyone
works well with teenage young people. Some adults who
offer to help should be steered to other ministry opportunities within the church. And others who've never offered
their services should be actively pursued to work with the
kids. The administrative team screens, recruits and as-
signs adults to help in youth ministry roles. Chapter 7
includes additional details about recruiting adult helpers.

4. Training. The administrative team is responsible for
training the adults who work with youth, and for the
youth who lead other youth. If they have the necessary
expertise, members of the administrative team may do
the training themselves. If not, they will need to call in
other resource people to provide training. The training
should include a full orientation on the youth-based ministry approach.

5. Appointing key people. The administrative team
may appoint individuals to the temporary planning task
force. Young people on the temporary planning task force
may be selected by the administrative team or elected by
the youth group. The adults on the planning task force,
however, should be appointed by the administrative team.
These adults should be chosen according to their understanding and support of youth-based ministry philosophy.

Also, the administrative team should select an adult
who will chair the steering committee, which handles the
ongoing business of the youth group. This steering com-

mittee is made up of youth and adults and is in many ways the backbone of youth-based ministry. The adults who serve on this committee have the power to "make or break" youth-based ministry. Therefore, this appointment must be handled with great care. See Chapter 9 for more details on the role of the steering committee and its chairperson.

6. Evaluating. The administrative team observes the progress of the youth ministry and offers suggestions for improvement. These evaluation duties usually include assessments of adult volunteer workers. The administrative team determines whether specific volunteers should be invited to serve another term. The team also is charged with the unfortunate responsibility of "firing" a volunteer whose behavior has a negative influence on the kids.

The administrative team also tracks the kids' progress and performance within the youth-based model. Our administrative team noticed that the young people had gradually slipped away from using certain elements they earlier had determined needed to be included in every youth group meeting. The administrative team pointed out this inconsistency and reminded the steering committee members of their careful work that had led to their earlier decisions about the group meeting formula.

7. Interpreting the youth ministry to the congregation. Youth-based ministry relies on a lot of communication. Church leaders and congregation members become easily dismayed if the youth ministry's successes and little failures aren't carefully interpreted to them. This is often the role of the administrative team.

In a church Thom attended many years ago, the youth ministry began attracting previously unchurched "street kids." Church kids evangelized their friends. The youth group grew—and these previously unchurched kids began bringing their parents to Sunday morning worship. But these were not the clean-cut kids (and parents) this church was accustomed to. The senior pastor and some of the congregational leaders began to quietly grumble. Some feared that the "riffraff" would have a negative influence on the "good" churched kids.

No one from the youth ministry bothered to (or even thought to) explain to the church leadership the wonderful progress that was being made with these "rough" kids. Left to their own interpretation of this youth-based ministry, the church leadership grew more and more negative. Then, one afternoon the senior minister overheard from his office a teenage boy blurt an obscenity during a car-wash fund raiser taking place in the church's parking lot. The senior minister repeated his ear-witness account to several congregational leaders. And soon the entire youth ministry was called into question. Eventually it crumbled, partially due to misinformed, unnecessarily hostile church leadership.

An administrative team was needed to serve as an advocate for the youth ministry. This team must confront in firm and loving ways any bad attitudes toward youth ministry. The kids need advocates to guard them from negative people.

In our current church, our administrative team spends considerable time educating the church leadership and congregation about the goals and workings of our youth-based ministry. The administrative team chairperson is a voting member of the churchwide council, which requires time and effort. The effort pays off.

8. Providing continuity. Many youth ministries disintegrate after a change of leadership. This is largely unnecessary. A strong administrative team provides stability and continuity during transitions of paid youth ministers, volunteer adults and key teenage leaders. The administrative team, with its knowledge of the youth ministry, can step in and assure that the youth-based model continues with few gaps. And since long-term planning is one of its key responsibilities, the administrative team should anticipate and plan for the ministry's needs six months from now as well as six years from now.

9. Encouraging the planning task force and steering committee. Young people and adults working on various youth ministry tasks can become discouraged. Temporary setbacks can deflate enthusiasm. Here's where the administrative team can step in and remind everyone of the ministry's goals and its good progress.

Creating Youth Visibility in the Church

Your youth-based ministry enhances its growth potential through heightened visibility in the church. It's worth your administrative team's effort to make your young people and the youth ministry program very conspicuous to your entire congregation—and to visitors.

Why is visibility important? It attracts young people to youth ministry programs. If kids consistently see their peers actively involved in the life of the church, they're more likely to follow suit.

High youth ministry visibility also serves as an effective church growth tool. Many church-shopping families choose churches with solid youth ministries. They're concerned about their children's spiritual growth. They often choose churches where young people and youth programs are in evidence on Sunday morning. Youth ministry visibility promotes evangelism.

And, good youth ministry visibility reinforces to your congregation its commitment to youth. People need reminders of their priorities and goals.

Building youth ministry visibility requires the commitment and cooperation of young people, parents, youth workers and church leaders. Here's a potpourri of ideas to get you started.

✔ **Reserve a pew for youth.** Ask all of your young people to sit together, in the front pew, for Sunday morning worship. A consolidated pack of kids makes a greater visual impact than the scattered look of random seating. The front pew draws maximum attention. Plus, the preacher gets a close-up weekly reminder of his youth constituency.

✔ **Musical presentations.** Youth choirs and youth solos provide fine visibility. Fifteen-year-old Corry did a beautiful piano solo during the offering at our church. People talked about it for months.

✔ **Graphic appeal.** When placing posters for upcoming youth events, don't confine them to the youth room down the hall. Seek permission to mount them in locations where all parishioners will see them. And, be sure announcements and reports of youth activities appear regularly in the general church newsletter and in bulletins, even if you also have a special youth newsletter.

✔ **Worship service servants.** Make sure young people regularly serve in visible Sunday morning roles: greeting, ushering, etc.

✔ **Support from the top.** Your senior pastor plays a key role in the success of youth-based ministry. His or her positive comments from the pulpit often elicit congregational support for the youth ministry. Conversely, even his or her mere silence can raise people's suspicions and damage the youth ministry's image. Meet regularly with your senior minister to explain youth ministry happenings. Urge him or her to mention the youth ministry publicly, perhaps even using anecdotes from your youth-based ministry as illustrations in sermons. Your young people need to feel support from the top.

✔ **Guest announcement-makers.** Young people at

our church are allowed to make brief Sunday morning announcements about youth ministry events and projects. They've become quite creative, sometimes using amusing skits—complete with costumes. Most congregation members look forward to these lighthearted times. Of course, there are those who believe that only pastors should make announcements. We're working on educating those individuals about the many benefits of building youth visibility in the church.

Education is often the first step toward committing your church to strengthening itself through greater youth ministry visibility. The administrative team plays the key role in keeping the congregation educated and informed about youth-based ministry.

CHAPTER SIX

The Planning
Task Force

*I*n order to get youth-based ministry moving in your church, we recommend using a temporary planning task force. This planning task force meets for several weeks or months to build a youth ministry structure best suited to your young people's needs.

The planning task force, comprised of a few young people and adults, evaluates your current youth ministry, assesses needs, builds a "constitution" for the new ministry and makes plans for the first few months of programming. This small group's primary task is to draw a game plan, mobilize people and resources for the new beginnings, and then kick off the ministry. Its goal is to establish a starting point for the new youth-based ministry.

Selecting the Task Force

When putting together your planning task force, keep in mind that a well-selected small group will help you move more efficiently than a large group. A planning task force of six to eight members is plenty large enough. Add any more, and you no longer have a "small group." This means people won't feel as comfortable to share openly, your planning process will take much longer, and the group's decisions will be diluted with unnecessary and excessive compromises.

More than one-half of the planning task force should be young people. Put into practice immediately the youth-based philosophy of granting large doses of responsibility to the young people. A planning task force populated primarily by adults tends to stifle kids—even if the adults keep relatively quiet.

Teenage members of the planning task force may be elected by the youth group or selected by the administrative team. Whether electing or selecting, here are some qualifications to consider:

■ The young people should be willing and able to meet frequently to accomplish the important work of the planning task force. They should agree to commit themselves to an effort that involves a lot of time and hard work.

■ They must agree to take a fresh-start approach to the new youth ministry. No "baggage" from past groups allowed.

■ Include a young person from each grade level, if possible. Sophomores often have different viewpoints than seniors.

The selection process of adults for the planning task force is crucial. The administrative team needs to approach this responsibility with great care. Appointing a loud, take-charge adult to the planning task force could douse the kids' enthusiasm and destroy the foundation for a healthy youth-based ministry.

Let's take a look at some of the considerations for placing adults on the planning task force:

■ Include your key adult (professional or volunteer) who oversees high school youth ministry.

■ Select one or two other adults with experience or interest in the youth ministry. Again, avoid overloading the planning task force with adults.

■ We don't recommend using youth group members' parents on the planning task force, especially if the parents' own kids are on the team. No matter how healthy a parent-teen relationship may be, a young person talks and acts differently when his or her parent is in the room. Young people should feel absolutely free to speak their minds at these meetings. We'll discuss this issue more in the next chapter.

■ Adults on the planning task force must agree to start fresh with a new youth ministry. Avoid selecting adults with the "good old days" mind-set.

■ Choose adults who embrace the youth-based ministry philosophy. Make sure they understand their role: *to help the young people form their own ministry*. Adults who love to push their own ideas on the youth group should be avoided.

You'll find more information on selecting the right adults for youth-based ministry in the next chapter.

Calling the Task Force Together

Members of the planning task force carry a crucial responsibility. Their decisions will have far-reaching consequences. So, it's important to approach these people and their time together with a dose of special treatment. Let them know how important they are!

Perhaps you'll want to begin your series of planning task force meetings with a special dinner—at your house or at a restaurant.

Spend ample time at your first session getting acquainted or reacquainted. Work on building unity and closeness within the planning task force. Your task force members need to feel very comfortable with one another. They need to trust each other—to know that they can speak candidly without being ridiculed. Perhaps most of your time spent in the first meeting will be in community-building and trust-building exercises.

Continue to use community-building activities each time your planning task force meets. Your planning will go smoother and your team members' enthusiasm for the new youth ministry will grow. Your community-building experiences needn't be fancy. You might begin a planning meeting by asking, "What's something good that has happened in your life this week? What do you thank God for? I'll start and we'll go around the circle." Or, you might ask the members to tell a little story about their names— where their names came from, what their names mean, what they were almost named, or funny things about their names. Or, you might ask members to share something they really admire about the person on their right. Denny Rydberg's book *Building Community in Youth Groups* (Group Books) includes scores of activities that will help form cohesiveness and build trust within your task force.

The atmosphere of the meeting room also can influence your task force. Arrange your chairs in a circle for your planning meetings. Make sure everyone is on the same eye level. This enhances intimacy and reinforces the youth-based philosophy of group process and shared responsibility.

One of your adults on the planning task force, usually the key youth ministry person, should act as the chairperson and prepare an agenda for each planning meeting. This adult also leads the meetings. "Why not name a young person as planning task force chairperson?" you may ask. Because young people, at this point, generally have no idea what to place on the agenda. And the planning meetings offer a wonderful opportunity for a skilled adult to model good group leadership. The young people can observe this leadership and later use what they've learned to lead youth group activities.

Even though an adult will facilitate these meetings, the kids will clearly see they're making the decisions. One of their first decisions will be to determine how often to meet. At our church, our planning task force met weekly for 90 minutes for four months. Your planning process may move faster—or slower—than ours. You may choose to concentrate your planning time during a weekend retreat.

Evaluating Your Needs

Near the top of the planning task force's agenda should be a review of your current youth ministry, if one exists. Go back and look at the results of the "Sack Poll" and the "Confidential Questionnaire" for inactive youth described in Chapter 3. Note any trends that emerge from this data.

Also, conduct a needs analysis among your church's young people. Planning new directions for your youth ministry must be based on good information, not guesses. In order for your ministry to meet needs you must be certain about what those needs are.

Your planning task force can assess fairly well your young people's needs through surveys. Charts 8, 9 and 10 are sample needs and interests inventories for your kids to complete. You may adapt or combine them to fit your young people. Be careful not to make any one survey look too long or too difficult to fill out. Remember to maintain confidentiality concerning the survey responses.

CHART 8
Youth Needs Survey 1

We're making plans for upcoming youth group programs. We want these programs to address your needs. But before we can address them, we need to know what they are. Help us by completing the following survey.

1. What are the top five worries or concerns in your life? (Check five only.)

_____ My relationship with God.

_____ Making and keeping friends.

_____ Peer pressure.

_____ Drugs.

_____ Drinking.

_____ Doing well in school.

_____ Dealing with temptation.

_____ My looks.

_____ The future.

_____ College.

_____ Nuclear war.

_____ World hunger.

_____ Dating.

_____ Racism.

_____ Money.

_____ My parents might die.

_____ I might kill myself.

_____ Loneliness.

_____ Stress.

_____ Cliques.

_____ Divorce.

_____ Self-esteem.

_____ Prayer.

_____ Getting along with parents.

_____ Music.

_____ Suicide.

_____ Sharing my faith.

_____ Cults.

_____ Other:_____

_____ Other:_____

2. The biggest issue or concern in my life right now is _____

THANK YOU!

CHART 9
Youth Needs Survey 2

We're making plans for upcoming youth group programs. We want these programs to address your needs. But before we can address them, we need to know what they are. Help us by filling in the blanks to the following statements.

1. One thing that really upsets me is _____.

2. One thing I wish I could change about myself is _____

_____.

3. One thing I would change about my parents is_____

_____.

4. My life would be better if _____.

5. If I could ask God one question, I'd ask _____.

THANK YOU!

CHART 10
Youth Needs Survey 3

We're making plans for upcoming youth group programs. Help us make these plans by telling us which topics interest you. Circle a number for each item.

	INTERESTS ME										NO INTEREST
Getting along with parents.	10	9	8	7	6	5	4	3	2	1	0
Alcoholic parents.	10	9	8	7	6	5	4	3	2	1	0
Single-parent households.	10	9	8	7	6	5	4	3	2	1	0
Stepparents.	10	9	8	7	6	5	4	3	2	1	0
Making friends.	10	9	8	7	6	5	4	3	2	1	0
Relating to non-Christian friends.	10	9	8	7	6	5	4	3	2	1	0

	INTERESTS ME									NO INTEREST	
What to do on a date.	10	9	8	7	6	5	4	3	2	1	0
How to be attractive to the opposite sex.	10	9	8	7	6	5	4	3	2	1	0
On a date, how far is too far?	10	9	8	7	6	5	4	3	2	1	0
How do I know God's will for my life?	10	9	8	7	6	5	4	3	2	1	0
What does "born again" really mean?	10	9	8	7	6	5	4	3	2	1	0
Why does God let bad things happen?	10	9	8	7	6	5	4	3	2	1	0
Coping with stress at school.	10	9	8	7	6	5	4	3	2	1	0
Cliques.	10	9	8	7	6	5	4	3	2	1	0
How to love myself.	10	9	8	7	6	5	4	3	2	1	0
Why doesn't God answer my prayers?	10	9	8	7	6	5	4	3	2	1	0
Is it wrong for Christians to drink?	10	9	8	7	6	5	4	3	2	1	0
How can Christians react to the nuclear threat?	10	9	8	7	6	5	4	3	2	1	0
Dealing with temptation.	10	9	8	7	6	5	4	3	2	1	0
What can we do about world hunger?	10	9	8	7	6	5	4	3	2	1	0
Dealing with peer pressure.	10	9	8	7	6	5	4	3	2	1	0
What will I do after high school?	10	9	8	7	6	5	4	3	2	1	0
What college should I attend?	10	9	8	7	6	5	4	3	2	1	0
What can I do about loneliness?	10	9	8	7	6	5	4	3	2	1	0
I'm scared of losing someone close to me.	10	9	8	7	6	5	4	3	2	1	0
What position should I take on abortion?	10	9	8	7	6	5	4	3	2	1	0
I worry about money.	10	9	8	7	6	5	4	3	2	1	0
Other:_____	10	9	8	7	6	5	4	3	2	1	0
Other:_____	10	9	8	7	6	5	4	3	2	1	0

THANK YOU!

Strive to get full participation in your needs analyses. Our planning task force chose to "bribe" kids to complete the survey. After church services one Sunday, the planning task force kids set up a table covered with plates of fresh brownies. They lured the high-school-age kids to the table with the brownies. Then they said, "Take the survey and win a brownie." The ploy worked. Except some kids wanted to take the survey over and over.

The results of your survey should supply the planning task force with plenty of ideas for constructing the future of your youth ministry. You'll be better equipped to set some goals, and you'll know some of the pressing issues that need to be addressed in your programming.

Designing Your Youth Ministry Foundation

The planning task force now begins to frame the "constitution" of your church's youth ministry. Many questions need to be answered and many far-reaching decisions need to made. What is the youth ministry's purpose? Whom is the youth group for? When should the youth group meet? What will the kids do? How should the leadership structure be formed? What role do the adults in the group play?

All of this brainstorming, planning and decision-making needs to be carefully recorded. So, ask for a volunteer from the task force to be the recorder. This person will take careful notes, type the information and distribute copies to all task force members.

1. Establish a purpose. What is the purpose of your youth ministry? Why should it exist? Ask for ideas and write all of them on a blackboard or large sheet of newsprint. Here's the list our planning task force made:

To help youth grow spiritually.

To allow youth to share problems.

To learn more about the Bible.

To build Christian friendships.

To provide fun activities that are Christ-centered.

To build self-esteem.

To help give youth a vision for the future.

To have time to get away and be with other kids.

To just have fun.

To give kids tools to cope with problems.

To help youth make good decisions as Christians.

To have a chance to serve or give.

To learn how to share faith.

To make God real to youth.

To help youth express their talents.

To help youth learn more about life.

To influence church worship services.

Once you see everyone's ideas for the purpose of the ministry, ask each planning task force member to write a statement of purpose. It may be a sentence or a short paragraph. Then ask each person to read aloud his or her statement. From these suggestions, press for a consensus on one statement that pleases the entire planning task force.

Point out that this purpose statement is important to the group in many ways. It will set the tone for future planning. And other people, even years from now, may refer to it and say something like, "That idea sounds okay, but does it really fit the purpose of our group?"

2. Determine a member profile. Ask, "Whom is our group for?" Seem too obvious? Consider these questions:

■ Is the group for high school kids only? junior high and senior high combined? combined all the time—or just on special occasions? What about kids who have graduated from high school but still want to be involved?

■ When is someone considered old enough to join the

group? In June, after they've completed ninth-grade? Or, do ninth-graders have to wait until September before joining the high school group?

■ Do we design the group based on the interests of the kids in our church? Or, do we plan things that will make our group appealing to unchurched kids? How will our regular members feel if a lot of non-Christian kids start coming? How will the church leaders feel if the non-Christian kids aren't the type of kids they want hanging around our "good" church kids? (These types of questions need to be addressed. Real evangelism often has a price that some churches aren't willing to pay.)

3. Form a schedule. Your planning task force should work out a structure and schedule for youth group meetings and functions. Should your group meet weekly? twice a week? biweekly? monthly?

What is the best possible day of the week for your young people to meet? We know many youth groups that have met for years on Sunday nights. When asked why, they said, "I don't know. Because we always have, I guess." Maybe Tuesday or Thursday night is best for your young people. Poll your members.

And, what time should your meetings begin? Is 7 p.m. best? Or would 6 p.m. be better? Or maybe your meetings should begin at 5 p.m. and culminate with a 6:30 p.m. snack supper. Weigh all the advantages and disadvantages.

Should your meetings last an hour? 90 minutes? two hours?

Where should your meetings be held? In the church basement every week? Or, should they be moved to members' homes occasionally?

4. Design formats for meetings and schedules. Your planning task force should determine at this stage the composition of your youth group meetings and other activities.

Time spent now, carefully considering what makes a meeting or program successful, will reap big benefits later.

Here's the list of meeting ingredients that our planning task force developed:

1. Community-building experience.
2. Singing.
3. "Learning part"—the lesson content.
4. Affirmation experience.
5. Prayer.
6. Specific closure experience.
7. Refreshments.

Our planning task force determined these ingredients to be essential. That is, each time our group meets, each of these elements must be included. The task force allowed for flexibility by specifying that the ingredients could be done in any order, and two or more may be combined. (See a full explanation of these seven ingredients in Chapter 12.)

Your planning task force may choose to be more defined—or more open—about your youth group meeting format. Discuss how to maintain quality but still allow for variety and surprises.

Next, the task force should consider a possible rhythm for your youth ministry programming. For instance, our planning task force decided to schedule regular weekly meetings and one special function every month. In lieu of a weekly meeting, a "special" might be a party, a lock-in, a Christian concert, miniature golfing, roller skating, swimming or a video movie night at a member's home.

Shaping a rhythm now will later help your steering committee fill the calendar without worrying about the group getting too studious or too socially oriented.

Now is also the time to discuss the inclusion of big

events in your annual calendar. Should the group plan a summer trip every year? What about retreats?

5. Design a steering committee. After the temporary planning task force finishes its work, you'll need an ongoing team of youth and adults to plan programs and handle administrative decisions. We call this team the steering committee.

The planning task force should decide the "shape" of the steering committee. How many young people should serve on it? Should each class be represented on the steering committee (e.g., two sophomores, two juniors, two seniors)? How and when will they be elected? How long will they serve? You'll find information to help answer these questions in Chapter 9.

6. Clarify the roles of adults. Youth-based ministry requires adults who are willing to let young people engage in decision-making. Not every adult makes a good youth-based ministry sponsor. Ask the planning task force to help determine the qualities that the administrative team should look for in adults. Explain that the adults will be screened and selected by the administrative team.

The planning task force kids at our church developed a list of desired qualities and possible duties of the people they call "adult helpers." Here's their list:

To help lead some activities.

To be "temporary parents."

To help supervise.

To support the group and its members.

To provide "crowd control."

To listen to youth.

To help with decisions.

To trust youth.

To share their faith.

NOT to take over!

The next chapter provides full information on the role of

adult helpers in youth-based ministry.

7. Consider names for the group. When launching a new youth-based ministry, you can draw attention to its newness by giving the youth group a new name. The entire group should select the new name, but the planning task force can speed things along by assembling a list of name nominations.

Names are important. A good name can build interest and conjure up positive images. A poor name can do the opposite. Urge the planning task force to think through how the name may sound to newcomers, parents and church leaders. You'll want a name that will still sound good next year, and the year after that. Consider traditional names such as "Christian Youth Fellowship" as well as more creative ones such as "God Squad" or "Sunday Night Special."

8. Solidify your "constitution." Your planning task force will be working hard to build the foundation for your youth ministry. Unless certain steps are taken, much of this effort may dissolve in time. And that's unfortunate and counterproductive. How will you safeguard against this? For example, your planning task force may spend hours determining that the steering committee should include six youth. Then, a year from now, someone may think 10 should be elected, because "fewer feelings would be hurt." And, in an emotional moment, the group may hastily overturn the planning task force's careful decision.

So, the planning task force may wish to build in some stability and longevity to its decisions. Perhaps your team will require that its foundational decisions need a two-thirds majority vote by the group to overrule. Or, maybe your team's decisions should require a two-week deliberation time by the group—in order to avoid hasty, emotional decisions.

Also, be sure the planning task force's decisions are typed and assembled into a "constitution" or "bylaws" type of document. It's important to have a tangible record to refer to, rather than someone's memory.

Planning the Launch of the New Group

Once the basics are decided, the planning task force is ready to plot the first few months of the new group's life.

It is important to launch the new youth ministry schedule with a special kick-off event. This may be some sort of spectacular-sounding activity to attract as many kids as possible. The planning task force (or a special team that the task force appoints) should carefully select and design the kick-off event. This will be the group's big chance to attract and retain many new members. You'll find a complete discussion of the kick-off event in Chapter 8.

Also, the planning task force should organize and prepare the youth group meetings for the first three months or so. This will give the new steering committee a chance to get organized during that preplanned period.

Chapter 12 supplies you with guidelines for planning youth group meetings within the youth-based model.

Keeping the People Posted

While the planning task force works, it's vital to communicate with all the young people, parents, church leadership and congregation about progress being made. Without communication, rumors and nasty suspicions often arise. With communication, positive anticipation builds.

An adult representative from your planning task force should meet frequently with church leadership, updating them on the team's progress. Plan a parents meeting to reveal the details of your new youth-based ministry.

Include bits of news from your planning meetings in your church newsletter. Send "news releases" to your young people and to their parents. For example, as soon as you know the date of your kick-off event, begin promoting it.

Try to seek to involve kids who aren't on the planning task force. Use them on special committees. Our planning task force appointed a special committee to build a giant cardboard maze for our kick-off event. The maze was built from large appliance boxes. We selected two kids to serve on that committee who had rarely participated in previous youth ministry activities. Many people predicted these two kids couldn't be counted upon to participate actively in anything at church. But, they showed up to help build the maze and loved it! They came to the kick-off event and have been involved in the youth ministry ever since.

That's another example of the beauty of youth-based ministry. Involving young people in the planning and doing of youth ministry makes them feel wanted, needed and valuable.

CHAPTER SEVEN

Adult Helpers

Youth-based ministry relies on the quiet but essential involvement of caring adults.

The kids love Trudy. She really understands her role as a youth-based ministry adult helper. A week or so before each meeting, she phones the young people in charge of closing devotions. "How are your plans coming for the devotions?" she asks. "What do you have in mind?"

"Oh, I was thinking about doing something on forgiveness," the teenage voice on the phone says.

"That's a great idea!" affirms Trudy. "How will you do it?"

"I don't know exactly," says 16-year-old Erica.

Trudy then sets up a time for Erica to stop by her house and pick up a book of short devotionals. Erica finds one she likes on the topic of forgiveness and prepares for

Sunday night.

Later in the week, Trudy calls Erica again and asks how things are going.

Sunday night, toward the end of the meeting, Erica looks around nervously. This is her first experience leading the group. Trudy catches Erica's eye, smiles and nods at the teenager. Erica stands and hesitatingly ventures into her closing devotion. Trudy beams. Erica glances up and sees Trudy's encouraging smile. Her confidence renewed, Erica completes the devotion with a beautiful prayer.

After the meeting, Trudy seeks out Erica and gives her a big hug. "That was really good!" Trudy says.

"Do you really think so?" Erica asks. "I was so nervous."

"I looked around, and everybody was really with you, Erica. I could tell you were hitting home with them," Trudy says.

Erica leaves the church feeling great—about herself, about the group. And the other group members go home with a relevant thought about God's forgiveness.

The Qualities of a Good Adult Helper

Who makes a good adult helper in youth-based ministry? Perhaps your mind darts to the stereotypical image:

- Young (early 20s) married couple.
- Good-looking.
- Funny.
- Talented in guitar playing and song leading.

Let's take a look at each element of this cliché. First, good youth-based ministry adults need not be young. In fact, healthy youth-based ministries often intentionally recruit older people to serve. We know a 70-year-old woman who serves a youth ministry in our town. She greets everyone at the door and keeps a lookout for lonely and shy kids. The young people affectionately call her "Grandma." She's a careful listener. When kids need someone to "hear them out" on the big issues in their lives, they sit down with Grandma. Adults of all ages should be considered for youth-based ministry.

Should adults serving youth ministries be married? Many churches think so. "Young people need married couples as positive role models," church leaders often say. "Besides, we worry about a single, young man spending time on retreats with our maturing young daughters." Well, it's true our young people need good role models. But some of our kids will remain single for many years before they marry. Some will never marry. They need good role models too. And, it's a shame to lose the gifts of many good single adults because of fears about a few who may take advantage of young people. Those "bad apples" generally can be screened out. Youth-based ministry can use both married and single adults.

Must effective youth workers be good-looking? That stereotype is quickly dismissed by observing the adult youth workers who participate in events such as GROUP Magazine's workcamps. You'll see every imaginable size, shape and physique—skinny, fat, tall, short, beautiful and homely. All are attractive to young people, if the adults' hearts contain love and God's spirit.

All good youth workers are funny—right? Well, let's modify that to: All good youth workers have a sense of humor. They don't need to be comedians or clowns. But they do need to be willing to laugh at themselves, and they need to feel free to laugh along with the kids when they perform their inevitable adolescent antics.

Can you succeed in youth ministry without musical talent? Well, the fact is that most do. A GROUP Magazine survey of successful youth workers found that only 25 percent play the guitar or piano.

So much for the stereotypes. What are the real qualities to look for in adults who serve a youth-based ministry?

1. Mature faith. Spiritual growth flourishes through relationships. Jesus' ministry exemplified a relational, people-to-people approach. Youth-based ministry also depends on a relational, group-process approach to spiritual growth. Adults often sow God's seeds in the kids, who in turn sow God's seeds in other kids.

In youth-based ministry, the adults' sowing doesn't necessarily take the form of teaching or preaching. More often, it's role modeling and simple sharing of personal faith during discussions and casual conversations.

So, adults serving youth-based ministries should be secure and mature in their Christian faith. New Christians, though they may be eager to help in the youth ministry, may not be your best choices for adult helpers. They can, however, be effectively used for short-term duties such as driving and helping at special events.

2. Love for young people. Many of us love youth ministry because, among other reasons, we find adolescents interesting, fun and lovable. We're intrigued by this special stage of life in which major decisions about faith and values are made. However, not everyone shares our affinity. When seeking good adult helpers, look for people who enjoy teenagers. See if they laugh at adolescents' humor. Find out if they feel joyous when a teenager takes a step of growth. Make sure they take seriously kids' life traumas such as breakups with boyfriends and girlfriends.

Love is the key ingredient for people who work with youth. We often tell hesitant, potential volunteer adult helpers that an effective youth worker needs 5 percent skill and 95 percent love. We then ask these people to think back to the days when they were teenagers. "What is the strongest memory you have of your youth group leader?'' we ask. Rarely do they recall skillfully taught Bible studies or eloquently delivered speeches. What they do remember is the love shown them by a caring adult.

3. Respect for young people. Youth-based ministry, by its nature, requires high levels of respect for young people. Adults who say, ''Those kids don't know what they want,'' won't make it in youth-based ministry. Neither will those who say, ''I've got to tell those kids what to believe.'' Adults qualified to serve in a youth-based ministry perceive teenagers as intelligent people on the verge of adulthood. They believe young people can do great things if given the opportunity. They view teenagers as a vital part of the church today, not embryos for the church of tomorrow. They seek to show kids how to make good decisions, rather than telling them what to decide.

4. Secure in their own identity. Adults are sometimes attracted to youth ministry out of a quest to satisfy their own hidden needs. Some of these people are hazardous to youth-based ministry and should be avoided. They come in many ''flavors'':

● **The Controllers.** These authoritarian adults can't stand to be around young people without barking orders. Controllers typically grew up in very strict households and endured much order-barking themselves. They now have a pent-up lust for power and won't be satisfied until the youth group is doing things their way.

● **The Rescuers.** These adults derive their feelings of self-worth from protecting young people from every kind of perceived danger. To allow young people to fail would be unthinkable to them.

● **The Messiahs.** These adults' egos require a flock of adoring teenagers at their feet. Messiahs have a need to be admired as great leaders. They wouldn't consider relinquishing the spotlight to a kid.

● **The Martyrs.** They insist on doing everything—
even if it kills them. Their self-worth isn't based on *who*
they are, but on *what* they do. Martyrs need the pity of
others who notice how self-sacrificing they are.

● **The Lovelorn.** These adults use youth ministry to
receive love—from the kids. Their behavior is based not
on what's best for the young people, but on what will win
the kids' love.

● **The Lonely Hearts.** These people typically have
few, if any, friends their own age. They use the youth
group to gain a social life. They attempt to be the kids'
buddies instead of healthy adult role models.

The adults mentioned above are all needy people. They
may use the youth ministry to take, instead of to give.
Look for healthily secure adults to fill your youth ministry
positions.

Parents as Adult Helpers

The question frequently arises: "What about using parents of group members as adult helpers?" Generally, we
advise against it.

Several years ago, Thom sought adults to chaperone a
two-week youth group trip. Several people, including a
couple of kids, suggested the mother of one of the girls in
the youth group. The girl said she wouldn't mind if her
mom joined the trip. So, Mrs. Barker (not her real name)
became a chaperone.

The first couple of days of the trip went okay. Then
things began to deteriorate. Ellen, Mrs. Barker's daugh-
ter, grew more sullen each day. And Mrs. Barker became
irritable.

The other kids on the trip enjoyed their time away
from their parents. It was a time to be a little crazy with

their peers. But every time Ellen attempted to join in the harmless antics, Mrs. Barker pulled her aside and scolded her.

During evening group discussions, Ellen attempted to share openly from her heart, as the other kids did. But her candid remarks often drew a cold glare from her mother.

To make matters worse, the other kids grew impatient with Mrs. Barker's irritability and began giving Ellen a hard time about her mother.

The trip ended with many hurt feelings.

We believe the youth group is a healthy place for young people to test their wings of independence, away from the scrutiny of parents. Teenagers need such a Christian environment, regardless of the quality of their relationships with their parents.

Ellen felt cheated because her behavior was judged on a different level than the other kids, due to the presence of her mother. She soon learned that she needed to edit her comments during group discussions. That censoring benefited neither her nor the rest of the group.

Young people should feel free to talk openly in the group. Suppose a group discussion emerged on the subject of parents. Would any young person respond in the same way if his or her parent were present?

Also, adult helpers themselves need to feel free to share candidly in group discussions. How many parents would talk openly about their inner struggles if their own kids were sitting across the room?

And what happens if a parent adult helper doesn't work out? What if you're faced with asking a parent to withdraw from his or her position? How will that parent feel about the youth ministry? How will the parent's reaction to being dismissed affect his or her child in the group?

In fairness, we must say that we've observed a number

of parents who were positive youth group sponsors. But we still consider parental involvement at this level risky. Once the precedent is set by using one parent as a regular adult helper, how will you deny the position to other well-meaning, but obviously unqualified, parents who want to serve?

This is not to say that parents can't be used in youth-based ministry. They may serve in other very significant roles. We'll discuss these possibilities in Chapter 10.

The Appropriate Number of Adult Helpers

Before we overhauled the youth ministry at our church, adults actually outnumbered the kids at some activities. During an evaluation time, a young person said, "Sometimes I feel smothered by adults. Who's the group for, anyway?"

Our situation was unusual. Most churches have trouble finding enough adults who wish to serve the youth ministry.

Either dilemma—too many adults, or too few—endangers an effective youth-based ministry.

After studying hundreds of youth groups, we found that a ratio of one adult per five high-school-age young people seems to work well. This balance enables the young people to really feel responsible in a youth-based ministry, yet it still allows adequate adult guidance.

This ratio applies to the number of adults at any one youth group activity. You may, however, involve more adult helpers in your ministry by using different sets of adult helpers on a rotating basis.

Recruiting Adult Helpers

Gary really wanted to work with the youth group. He

pestered the youth minister for months. "I really want to serve the Lord, and I know he's calling me to use my gifts with the young people," said this 25-year-old.

The senior pastor told the youth minister, "I think it's great Gary wants to help the youth group. This would be a wonderful way to involve him in the church."

Finally, the youth minister let Gary serve as a volunteer youth worker. Almost immediately, the youth minister knew he'd made a mistake. Gary used his time with the kids to show off. He wore sleeveless shirts and walked on his hands to reveal his muscle-building accomplishments. He frequently interrupted serious discussions with inappropriate crudities. At first the kids seemed amused, but soon they tired of his selfish showmanship. Then, during a retreat, Gary offered marijuana to some of the kids.

"He just seemed so enthusiastic about our youth ministry," the youth minister said after he endured the unpleasant task of removing Gary from the youth ministry.

Gary's story brings us to the first rule of recruiting adult helpers: Don't accept just anyone who comes along. Many adults who volunteer do so in order to fulfill an inappropriate personal need.

Even though youth-based ministry promotes youth decision-making, the selection of adult helpers should not be left up to the kids. They're busy enough with their ongoing youth-based duties. Besides, screening adult helpers often involves disclosure of character traits and personality quirks. How many adults would allow their names to be placed in nomination if they knew a bunch of high school kids would be scrutinizing their positive and negative attributes? This information deserves to be handled confidentially by a small group of responsible adults (the administrative team).

We've discussed what to do if an unqualified person volunteers to serve. Another (and usually more common) problem is that many qualified adults do not volunteer. So, if many good adult helpers never volunteer and the kids shouldn't select adults, how do you go about recruiting? We must admit that finding and recruiting good adults is not an easy job. Quality—in anything—rarely comes without hard work. With that in mind, here are a few guidelines:

1. Always watch for potential candidates (even when all your volunteer positions are filled). Observe the behavior of various adults in your church as they interact with others. Keep notes on those adults who exhibit a mature faith, a love for kids, a healthy respect for young people, and whose personal needs are being met in appropriate ways.

2. Make appointments with potential candidates. Tell them you admire their gifts, and that you would like to explore how those gifts might be expressed in ministry. Conduct informal interviews. Do them in person, never over the phone. Some possible interview questions: How would you describe today's teenagers? What do they need most? How should adults help them meet those needs? When you think about working with young people, what appeals to you most? least?

Even if the interview really impresses you, don't ask for the person's commitment at that point. Mention that you'll be speaking with a number of potential adult helpers. Start building the image (and reality) that it's an honor to serve on the youth ministry team. Only the most qualified should be offered volunteer positions.

3. When possible, ask candidates to help out at a specific youth activity. Observe their interaction with the young people.

4. Ask potential adult helpers to complete the "Youth

Ministry Survey'' that appeared in Chapter 3. Scrutinize their responses.

5. Ask God's guidance in selecting adults who will best enable young people to grow closer to him.

6. When you've identified the best candidates, send them formal letters of call. Again, build the images of honor and importance. Chart 11 is a sample letter of call:

CHART 11
A Sample Letter of Call

Dear Robert,

As you may know, our church takes young people very seriously. They are a priority here. Our ministry with them is one of the most important in the church.

It is in this spirit that I'm writing you. In recent weeks we have grown in admiration of your gifts and abilities, Robert. We believe God has given you some personal tools that can be used to make a real difference in the lives of the young people here at First Church.

After a careful assessment and much prayer, the Youth Board of First Church of Hazeltown has unanimously chosen to call you for the position of Adult Helper with the high school youth group.

This volunteer position involves a three-month term, to begin August 1.

Bill Smith, our youth minister, will be speaking with you in the next few days to discuss the details of this position. Until then please pray about how God might use you to affect the lives of his children.

In ministries with youth,

Ann Jones
Chairperson
Youth Board

---

7. Call the candidate and make an appointment to talk. Again, do not conduct this talk over the phone. Explain fully the details and expectations of being an adult helper. Give the candidate a written job description of an adult helper's responsibilities. Discuss the concepts of youth-based ministry. Explain the term of service you're requesting. Chart 12 is a sample job description.

CHART 12
A Sample Job Description for Adult Helpers

You're a vital catalyst in the youth ministry here at First Church. Your tasks, no matter how insignificant some may seem, truly contribute to the personal growth of our young people.

In addition to the standard expectations of an adult helper (such as being a good role model), we have identified some specific tasks for you:

1. Contact four assigned young people weekly to verify that they have prepared their assignments for the Sunday night meeting.

2. Arrive at the church at 5:45 p.m. each Sunday. Help the youth set-up team arrange the chairs for the meeting.

3. Participate fully in meeting activities.

4. Help the set-up team return the chairs to the storage closet after the meeting.

5. After all young people have left the church, assure that all doors are locked.

6. Participate in special events such as retreats and fund-raising projects.

7. Attend monthly steering committee meetings.

8. Contact the steering committee youth reporter to verify that the minutes have been typed and placed in appropriate mailboxes.

9. If you are unable to attend a youth group function, call Jerry at 555-5793 a week in advance, if possible.

10. In all ministries that you perform, be open to God's power and grace, which will equip you to be the best you can be.

Term of Service

Vicky poured her energies into the youth ministry at our church. Whenever a job needed to be done, this 40-year-old woman took it on with fervor. She was wonderful! But after 18 months of service, she wrote the pastor a terse note: "I'm sorry, but I must withdraw my involvement in the youth ministry. It has consumed too much of my time. I've been denied adequate time for myself and my family. I see no end in sight if I stick with the youth group. I can't keep this up forever. I'm afraid I would give and give and give until there would be nothing left of me. I'm sorry."

Then there was Drew. He appeared to be a promising adult helper when he joined the youth-based ministry. But as time went on, he grew lazier and lazier. Although he attended every youth group meeting, he no longer made his assigned calls to kids to remind them of their responsibilities. "They're old enough to remember that stuff," he said. "I've got better things to do with my time than hand-holding a bunch of irresponsible teenagers." We were stuck with an adult helper who wanted to take part in the fun stuff but became resentful about the work involved in youth-based ministry.

And we remember Howard. He would have made a marvelous adult helper, but he refused to serve, saying, "I'd love to help, but I just don't think I can commit two years to this. That just seems like such a long time. What if I find out I'm not cut out for youth ministry? Or, what if I get too busy in a few months?"

The situations with Vicky, Drew and Howard could have been avoided by establishing specific terms of service. We recommend an initial term of three months for first-time adult helpers. Then terms may be renewed in six-month lengths.

Had this policy been in effect, Vicky's burnout and resentment could have been avoided. From her viewpoint, her youth ministry involvement looked endless and hopeless. She feared that her energetic involvement would sentence her to another 50 years of hard labor. Had she been enlisted for six-month terms, she could have seen an end to her service. She could have guiltlessly invested her energies, knowing that her responsibilities would end in just a few months. And she would have known she had the option to renew her commitment for another term if she had wished. In this way, she could have served happily without overworking herself into a burnout condition.

A limited term of service also would have tactfully handled the situation with Drew. During the initial trial term of three months, we would have seen that Drew was not working out. At the end of his term, we could have said, "Thanks, Drew, for serving your term. We appreciate your help. We may call on you again to help us out on retreats or trips."

Chances are, he would have been relieved. But if he would have asked about serving for another term of regular duty, we could have said, "We appreciate your willingness, Drew, but we have other people who want to serve, and we feel we need to give them a try too. Besides, the last three months have shown us that you serve best on special events such as retreats and trips. We all know that making those weekly phone calls to the kids was not something you enjoyed."

In Howard's case, a limited term of service probably would have appealed to him. He wasn't interested in an open-ended commitment. A defined term of service would have given him the security he needed. And, ironically, he probably would have renewed and served as long as most people.

Howard, and the rest of us, appreciate knowing exactly

what we're getting into. If the task sounds manageable, we're more likely to accept it. So, definite terms of service bring several benefits to youth-based ministry:

1. Specific commitment for all prospective adult helpers. Your volunteers aren't wondering, "Am I going to have to do this for the next 10 years?" You'll be able to recruit more good people.

2. A sense of hope. When youth work seems too tough, adult helpers serving defined terms are likely to say, "I can make it to the end of my term," rather than, "This is hopeless; I can't go on another day."

3. Burnout prevention. Before your volunteers burn themselves out, they're offered a break—gracefully. When their term is up, they've completed their commitment. There's no obligation to keep giving past their personal limits. In fact, you may choose to rotate your adult helpers to assure that they stay fresh and eager. Perhaps you'll want your adults to serve for six months, furlough for six months, then serve for another six months, and so on. Or, maybe you'll ask your adults to serve alternating months during their terms.

4. Affirmation for good work. Adult helpers who perform well are asked to serve another term. Whether or not they choose to accept, they're affirmed by being asked to renew their commitment.

5. Tactful recourse for poor performance. Adult helpers who perform poorly aren't asked to renew. They're thanked for serving, and they bow out with dignity. And remember, some adults, though they may be unqualified for regular service, may perform well at one-shot responsibilities such as lock-ins, trips, dinners and so on.

It is because of the danger of poor performance that we recommend giving a new adult helper an initial term of just three months. This allows enough time to evaluate performance, but isn't too long if the adult turns out to be unsuited for the responsibility.

Then, regular six-month terms seem to work well. Six months are long enough to provide a good measure of continuity, but short enough to sound manageable to the adult helpers.

Turnover of Adults

Now, you may say, "Six months? What if most adult helpers turn over that often? That provides little time for quality relationships to grow between the kids and adults. There's no continuity!"

Well, experience shows that most good adult helpers will renew for several six-month terms. Also, we must remember youth-based ministry's focus of continuity. It's not on the adults; it's on the young people! Many adults don't like to accept this change in focus, but it's key to your youth-based ministry's momentum and strength.

Counteract any lack of adult continuity by enriching the leadership and responsibilities among your young people. Let *them* provide the necessary continuity in your youth ministry. Use the youth-based models in this book, teach peer ministry skills, set up prayer partners and small support groups among your young people.

We agree, however, that constant turnover of adult helpers is unfortunate for any youth ministry. You can minimize undesirable impacts on your young people by staggering your adult helpers' terms. Start each of their terms on different months. This will prevent the possibility of an overnight "housecleaning" of your total adult team.

Roles of the Adult Helper

Youth-based ministry requires special qualities and expectations from adults. Let's look at some of the key elements:

● **Adult helpers participate fully with the group.** In many respects, adults are on the same level with the young people. They don't stand on the sidelines; they participate in all group activities, join in group games and mixers. They take part in group discussions. They're free to be vulnerable, to share deeply, to admit their mistakes and weaknesses. But they never use their adult clout to overtake or dominate a discussion or learning experience. And, since they're part of the group, adult helpers take their turns at the dirty work—setting up chairs, bringing refreshments, washing dishes, cleaning up, and so on. Young people respond positively to adults who are willing to be "real" alongside them.

● **Adult helpers understand group process.** Instead of hitting the kids with a 30-minute lecture on the evils of premarital sex, good adult helpers enable the group to explore the subject together. Perhaps the group will make two lists about premarital sex: one headlined "The Price," and the other headlined "The Payoff." The adults will then quietly guide the group discussion— making sure everyone has a chance to speak, drawing out the quiet ones. Soon the kids learn the process of looking at pros and cons, of listening to God's Word, of making good Christian decisions on their own.

● **Adult helpers know when to exert adult wisdom.** Although adult helpers relate to the young people as members of the group, they do not relinquish their adulthood. They use their maturity and wisdom in matters of safety. For example, if several kids head across an unsafe partially frozen river, the adults don't take time for a group discussion. They shout, "Stop!" and prevent an accident.

Adults also use their depth of experience to help guide

kids through unfamiliar issues. For instance, the kids may structure a lock-in with a serious learning experience at 3 a.m. Adults experienced with lock-ins should step in and ask the kids if they can think of a more effective time than 3 a.m.

● **Adult helpers share in successes and failures.** "We" is a big word in youth-based ministry. After the young people make a decision that results in a flop, the adult helpers should say, "Well, we missed it on that one." It's "we"—not "those kids" or "those other adult helpers"—even if the adults could have predicted the outcome before the kids made the ill-fated decision. Adults must be willing to face parents, church leaders and the congregation and share the blame for the group's failures.

The same principle applies to successes. There's little room in youth-based ministry for adults with bloated egos. When a success occurs, good adult helpers deflect any personal praise to the group at large.

● **Adult helpers know when to rescue.** Adults in youth-based ministry should recognize those rare circumstances when they must step in and save the young people from an irreparable failure. These dire circumstances include anytime the ongoing ministry to the entire group is jeopardized. For example, let's say the group has been planning a mission trip for a year. Twenty kids have planned their summer schedules around the trip. Two weeks before the trip, the group treasury is $1,000 short. In this situation, the adults may need to take action to raise the money, rather than cancel the trip.

Another example: 15-year-old Bobby forgets to bring the refreshments for the big Christmas party. In this situation, there's no need for the adults to rescue Bobby. The failure will be a good learning experience. Bobby will learn to be more responsible—and the group will learn forgiveness when someone lets them down.

An interesting phenomenon often occurs after youth-based ministry has been in effect for some time: The kids begin to rescue each other. For instance, kids in our youth group sometimes fail to prepare their responsibilities for youth group meetings. Several of our young people are watchful of this and step in themselves. They ad-lib and do a remarkable job of filling unexpected gaps in the meetings.

● **Adult helpers verify and remind young people of their responsibilities.** This is one of the essential keys to the success of youth-based ministry. Attempting youth-based ministry without a system of verification will almost certainly lead to collapse. Please carefully read and heed the advice in the following paragraphs.

Young people can handle impressive responsibilities in youth-based ministry. But they *are* teenagers. They are not yet adults. To expect them to perform as responsibly as mature adults is unrealistic and unfair.

Yes, you might ask one of your adult friends to prepare something for a church meeting that's six weeks away. And, yes, that friend should be expected to do his or her duty without further reminders. But we cannot expect all high school kids to follow through with similar responsibility without frequent encouragement.

So, let's say various young people in your group have agreed to plan and lead the different elements of your weekly youth group meetings. Each week, prior to the meeting, adult helpers should call each young person who is assigned a responsibility. The adults remind the kids of their duties, verify that they'll be at the meeting and ask if they need any help. If any young people sound unprepared, the adults should plan to call them again later in the week to check on progress.

Whenever we present this concept to adults, someone usually says, "All that calling and checking sounds like

nagging to me. Don't the kids resent it?'' No, not if it's
handled properly. In fact, the kids look forward to the
calls if the adults use skill and love. "I love it when
Stephanie calls,'' said 16-year-old Tom, a member of our
group. "She really cares.''

Stephanie, one of our adult helpers, uses the verification calls to build her relationships with the kids. She
doesn't begin her calls with, "Do you have everything
ready for Sunday night?'' She says something like,
"How's your week going? I heard you had a tennis match
on Monday. How'd it go?'' Eventually the conversation
turns toward the Sunday night responsibility.

Verification is time-consuming. But it's an essential duty
for adult helpers. So, be sure to distribute the work
among all your helpers.

● **Adult helpers prepare and direct agendas.** A
designated adult helper should prepare agendas for youth
group meetings, retreats and steering committee sessions. The young people may conduct various portions of
meetings and other activities, but one person needs to organize all the elements. This adult may then use a subtle
approach to advance the agenda and keep it on schedule.
For instance, 17-year-old Debbie may tend to lose track
of time when she directs group games and mixers. The
adult helper, ever watchful of the clock, merely smiles
and quietly taps his wristwatch when it's time to move
on. Debbie knows that's her cue to wrap up her activity.
The rest of the group, unaware of the cue, simply observes that youth-led meetings seem to stay on schedule.

On other occasions, the time-conscious adult helper
may pull aside young people and consult with them. For
example, upon observing that part of a meeting is running
long, an adult may whisper to the young person who's
next on the agenda: "We're running short on time. It
looks like we'll have time for only one song. Which one

do you want to sing?''
  ● **Adult helpers provide positive role models.**
Young people need adults in their lives who demonstrate
mature Christian behavior. They need to see how Christian adults respond to competition, injustice, frustration,
surprises, self-examination, fun times, sad times, faith and
doubt.
  We know an adult helper who models compassion and
outreach to "the least of these" among us. She spots
newcomers, loners and outcasts in the youth group and
does all she can to integrate them and make them feel
wanted and important. Several of the regular members
have watched her good example of Christian love and
have begun to emulate her efforts.

Adult Helper Training

  Few adults are "naturals" at youth-based ministry. All
need training before being incorporated into this special-
ized ministry with young people. Training builds adults'
effectiveness and confidence.
  Initial training can be done during a series of weekly
sessions, or at an all-day event, or on a weekend retreat.
Some elements to include in training:
  1. Community-building. Take time at the start of
your training to help your new adult helpers get to know
one another. Build a good level of trust from the very
beginning.
  2. A complete briefing of the goals and features of
youth-based ministry. You may use Chapter 2 as a basis
for this orientation.
  3. A thorough explanation of the role of an adult
helper. Use this chapter to help guide you through all the
responsibilities.
  4. An examination of the young people's role in youth-

based ministry.

5. An exploration of group process, discussion facilitation and Christian decision-making. (See Chapter 11.) Use role plays to allow your adult trainees to experiment with these skills.

6. Practical lessons on active listening and simplified counseling. A good resource to help you teach these skills is *Friend to Friend* by J. David Stone and Larry Keefauver (Group Books).

Training is an ongoing process; it is never completed. Continue to provide training for your adults through resources, seminars, conferences and consultations.

Firing an Adult Helper

Despite careful screening procedures and thorough interviewing we occasionally face the dismal reality that certain adult helpers are a negative influence on the group. They may display any number of inappropriate behaviors and attitudes:

● Boorish refusal to work with youth-based ministry philosophy.

● Shirking of responsibilities.

● Verbal, physical or sexual abuse of youth group members.

● Poor role modeling.

● Inability to work cooperatively with other adult helpers.

● Heretical theological positions.

When adult helpers display attitudes or behaviors that impede or endanger the youth ministry or the welfare of the young people, it's time to take steps to remove them. Does that sound harsh? Perhaps. But remember, our focus in youth-based ministry (in any youth ministry, really) is on the young people. When faced with difficult situations, we must always ask, "But what's best for the kids?"

We made the above statement at a recent seminar on youth-based ministry. A woman stood and defended her decision to allow an unqualified adult helper to remain on her team. "I know he has done a lot of stupid things. And the kids really don't want to have much to do with him," she said. "But this man has been through a lot of pain in his personal life. I just don't think it would be right to hand him one more dose of rejection."

We asked her to list the priorities of her youth ministry. She put "nurture the young people" at the top of the list. After citing many other priorities, we asked where on her list she would place "the personal satisfaction of adult helpers." "Toward the bottom," she admitted.

We praised her pastoral concern for the unsuitable adult helper. "We need to treat such individuals with love and tenderness," we said. "But we must not allow the priority of a secondary ministry to topple the priorities of our first ministry. The ministry to that man and the ministry to your kids both can be accomplished, but probably not within the same program. We would encourage you to find another place in your church where the man can become involved—where his involvement will not impede an existing ministry to other people."

Youth-based ministry is not designed to "sacrifice" young people for the sake of an adult. But churches are often slow to embrace this concept. For example, we know of many congregations that have retained unsuitable pastors for years. Is it because the people have not recognized how these pastors have impeded their congregations? No, they almost always admit they hired the wrong person for the job. They're willing to inflict continued suffering on the congregation because they love the minister and can't bear the thought of hurting his or her feelings.

People serving in the church need to think clearly about their priorities, write them down, and then stick to them. Enforcing our priorities may be painful at times. But we must do it out of love for those at the top of our lists. We have precedent for this: God sent his Son to lead us, to teach us, to minister to us. When his Son screamed from the cross, God could have chosen to spare him from that pain. But that was not his priority. You and I and the rest of Jesus' youth group were the priority. God made a tough decision because his love for us came first.

Out of love for your young people, sometime you will probably face the unpleasant task of dismissing an adult helper. How should you do it?

First, if the adult's behavior is marginal and is causing little more than an irritation, you may allow him or her to serve out the rest of the current term. Then offer your thanks for his or her service, but do not offer a renewal of service. Instead try to find another, more appropriate spot in the church for the person to serve.

If an adult's behavior is more serious, it may be time to take more immediate action. Discuss the situation with your administrative team. Pray about it. Then, if the adult's behavior cannot be corrected, begin the dismissal procedure. Make an appointment with the adult helper. Affirm him or her as a person of value. Offer your thanks for his or her work. Then explain why you have determined that a dismissal is in order. Cite specific examples of inappropriate behavior.

Again, before your dismissal talk, try to find a more appropriate position within the church where the person can serve. Offer and explain this position during the talk.

In many cases, an unsuited adult helper recognizes the same problems you've observed. If that's the case, the dismissal will be no surprise—and perhaps even a relief.

In other cases, the adult may become angry and defensive during the dismissal talk. Be prepared for this. Don't argue. Simply state your reasons for your decision and allow the person to be angry. But do not apologize for your decision. Conclude the conversation with words of love. Then follow up later by writing a loving, personal note and/or taking the person to lunch. It's crucial to communicate that you still love the worker and consider him or her a person of value.

Never share details of this personnel problem with the young people. Simply state that the youth ministry administrative team felt that the adult is better suited to serve elsewhere in the church.

And remember, we sometimes must make tough decisions in order to provide the best ministry for our young people.

CHAPTER EIGHT

The Kick-Off Event

*T*he chances of success for your new youth-based ministry can be greatly enhanced by giving your young people a good first impression. That's why we recommend putting a lot of energy into a kick-off event, the first program your kids will experience under youth-based ministry.

When we kicked off youth-based ministry at our church, we built a gigantic human-size cardboard maze. It was so intricate that kids spent about 20 minutes inside trying to find their way out. The same evening the kids also built "the world's largest banana split." We used a 10-foot-long rain gutter as our dish. Our kick-off was well-attended, and it established the new youth ministry as creative, fun and youth-based.

A kick-off event seeks to accomplish several objectives:

★ It draws attention to the new youth ministry. It signals a new start. It makes a good first impression in order to draw continued attendance.

★ It models the new youth-based approach. Young people lead the activities.

★ It serves as a pre-evangelism tool. The appealing program may attract not only your regular church kids, but unchurched kids too.

★ It offers an opportunity to preview upcoming youth ministry meetings, events, projects and programs.

★ It provides a good number of young people to vote on the new steering committee members, if you wish.

Key Elements

Good kick-off events include a number of essential ingredients:

1. The event must be attractive. Search for a concept that sounds really fun and unusual. The kick-off event is intended to grab attention.

2. Include opportunities during the event for young people to get acquainted with one another. GROUP Magazine surveyed young people about why they attend youth groups. The number-one answer: to make friends. Use the kick-off event to help satisfy young people's need for relationships. Plan mixers, community-building exercises and informal time.

3. Take time during the kick-off event to preview the new youth-based ministry. Have teenage members of your planning task force explain how youth-based ministry works. They also should present "teasers" about upcoming meetings and activities. Make this a fun time; use homemade slide shows or videos, funny skits, props and posters.

4. Hand out fliers and calendars that promote upcoming

events. Design these attractively so the kids will be inclined to post them on their bulletin boards at home.

5. Be sure to include a spiritual emphasis—a brief worship or devotional. Today's young people are hungry for spiritual direction. A well-prepared, meaningful moment at your kick-off event will leave your kids wanting more.

6. Some optional activities: Elect your new steering committee. Vote on the group's new name. Decide the destination of the next big group trip. If time permits, these decisions can serve to illustrate youth-based ministry in action and build more anticipation for the future.

Selecting the Right Kick-Off Event

This is a big decision. Your planning task force should spend considerable time exploring and evaluating different kick-off event options. Consider these criteria:

1. Does the idea sound fun and exciting to young people? If in doubt, poll the kids in your church for their opinions.

2. Would this idea be universally appealing? Many events can be ruled out here. For instance, a dance may be a poor choice because many kids don't like to dance. Caution your planning task force members to select an event that's not their own personal favorite, but one that would be attractive to everyone.

3. Can the event be done at the church? We believe it's important to kick off your new ministry in the same place where your regular meetings will be held. In this way, you build familiarity and a positive mental image of your regular meeting place.

4. Does the event offer ample time for kids to get acquainted with each other? This may rule out a concert or a video night.

5. Select the best possible date. Carefully research

kids' calendars to find a date with the fewest conflicts. There are few things more heart-breaking than pouring dozens of hours into an event, then having only two kids show up because it was scheduled on the night of the state basketball championship.

There are probably hundreds of good kick-off events from which to choose. Here are a few examples:

1. A human-size maze. Connect large cardboard appliance boxes to build a giant crawl-through maze. Put in plenty of twists and dead ends. Hide several scary-costumed kids in dark corners to "terrorize" passersby. Turn out the lights and send kids through on their hands and knees. They love it! Find a complete description of this activity in *The Youth Group How-to Book* (Group Books).

2. Pizza-eating contest. Make several varieties of pizza and see who can eat the most pizza in a minute. To complicate things, allow no use of hands during the competition.

3. Air band competition. Ask kids to prepare lip-sync acts to their favorite records.

4. Exotic meal. Prepare a dinner with a special flair—Hawaiian luau, chili cook-off, Mexican fiesta, etc.

5. World's largest whatever. Build a giant banana split, ice cream sundae, submarine sandwich or pile of nachos.

Publicity

The kick-off event determines the early success of your youth-based ministry. So, give special attention to publicizing this big event. Go all out. Here are some suggested strategies:

★ **Mailings.** Young people love to receive mail. Capitalize on this fact by sending announcements of the upcoming event. But don't just send a letter. Think creatively! If you're holding an air band contest, send your announcements in paper bags. Tell the kids to blow up their sacks and bring their air to the contest. If you're having a giant maze, send a poster with an intricate maze puzzle on it. Tell the kids to solve the maze puzzle and bring their posters with them to receive special prizes. If you're having a luau, send everyone a plastic lei.

★ **Posters.** Appoint a special committee to create some wild posters. Put them up wherever you can, including some unexpected places (in hallways, on ceilings, in lavatory stalls, and so on).

★ **Mystery box.** Decorate a large (3'×3'×3') cardboard box. Tack six-foot-long 1"×2" boards inside each corner. Stand the unit on its legs, with the box, open side down, atop the legs. Post creative notices of the kick-off event on the inside of the box. Curious kids will need to bend over and pop up inside the box in order to read the "mystery message." Place the unit in a high-traffic area in your church.

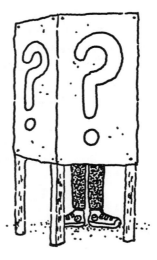

★ **Spoken announcements.** Ask for time during your Sunday morning worship services to allow youth representatives to make announcements about the kick-off event. Our kids created short (one- to three-minute) skits and presented them to the entire congregation. They were very clever, and they not only accomplished their intended purpose, but they promoted good public relations throughout the congregation.

★ **Phone calls.** Use a personal touch; contact each potential youth group member by phone. Form a special calling committee. Divide the membership roster among committee members and keep calling till everyone personally has been invited.

★ **Buttons.** Make up a catchy slogan such as "Join the group," "The dream begins here" or "Super Sunday." Put the slogan on pin-backed buttons and have your planning task force members wear them for several weeks. They'll get asked many questions about the mysterious slogan which will give your task force members opportunities to talk about the kick-off event. (Button-making kits are available, economically, from Badge A Minit, Civic Industrial Park, Box 800, LaSalle, IL 61301.)

★ **Parents meeting.** Conduct a special parents meeting prior to your kick-off event. Explain the new youth ministry and ask for the parents' support. Urge them to encourage their teenagers to attend the kick-off event.

Publicity is crucial. Don't just use one method. Use all of the above strategies, plus any others you come up with.

Follow-Up

At your kick-off event, be sure to obtain every attendee's name, address and phone number. Place a guest book near the door where the kids will come in. Station an adult and a young person at the table. They ask everyone to sign in. Use this list to follow up on the kick-off event. Send each of the members a letter, thanking them for coming. Include duplicate copies of the calendars and fliers that were handed out at the event. (You can be sure that many of these were lost on the way home from the kick-off event.) Insert an enticing invitation to the next meeting, reminding them of the time and place. Encourage them to bring friends.

Also, do a mailing to all those who did not attend the kick-off event. Include the announcements of upcoming activities and urge them to become involved.

CHAPTER NINE

The Steering
Committee

*O*nce your planning task force has completed its
work and your new youth-based ministry is
launched, you'll need a team of kids and adults who will
help guide the group on an ongoing basis. We call this
team the "steering committee."

The steering committee is, in many ways, the "nerve
center" of a youth-based ministry. Though the administrative team supervises the entire youth ministry, it's the
steering committee that actually forms the plans and creates much of the programming. Let's take a look at this
team's crucial duties:

1. Setting priorities. The steering committee oversees the youth ministry program and continually evaluates
its goals and performance. This team struggles with some
tough questions: Are we successfully encouraging Chris-

tian growth among our group members? Do we have a good balance of nurture and outreach? How are we ministering to inactive youth in our church? Is our ministry attractive to unchurched young people? How much time should we devote to fun activities versus spiritual growth programs? How well are we involving all the kids in the group?

2. Planning. The steering committee tackles the tough job of planning future youth group meetings, programs, projects, retreats and special events. Once plans are initiated, the steering committee often delegates responsibilities to other young people or task forces.

3. Setting policies. Like any organization, youth ministry needs rules, guidelines and procedures in order to operate smoothly. The steering committee makes many policy decisions itself, and refers others to the whole youth group.

4. Handling discipline problems. A few young people in any group will always challenge the authority and break the rules. Many of these cases are best handled by the rule-breakers' peers—the kids on the steering committee.

Size and Makeup of the Committee

How many young people and adults should serve on the steering committee? We recommend keeping this team small. Group process begins to erode with more than eight people. Your steering committee will feel freer to talk openly in a small group. A larger group will slow the committee's progress and diminish its ministry potential.

Most groups elect one or two representatives from each class to serve on the steering committee. This plan assures better representation than if members were simply elected at large. It also trains your younger members in leadership skills, which in turn creates greater continuity in later years.

The steering committee should be chaired by an adult who is chosen by the administrative team. This chairperson is often the key adult for high school youth ministry. He or she carries several responsibilities:

1. Calls steering committee meetings and reminds kids to attend.

2. Prepares agendas for all meetings.

3. Brings resources and ideas to the meetings.

4. Keeps the meetings moving, starting and ending them on time.

5. Asks one of the young people to record, copy and distribute minutes for each meeting.

The chairperson also may invite other adult helpers to attend steering committee meetings. But, adults should never outnumber kids. And again, we advise against using group members' parents in this capacity.

Length of Term

Steering committee members usually serve for one year. Six months also would work, but we prefer 12 months. A one-year term allows committee members to plan a full year of programming, including any big summer plans.

Most groups elect their steering committee members at the beginning of the school year. This seems to be a natural transition point.

Selection of the Committee

Occasionally youth workers ask, "Why can't I just appoint (instead of elect) kids to the steering committee? I know which kids would do the best job." That's probably true, but once your youth-based ministry is instituted, it's crucial that young people see that they're trusted to make satisfactory decisions. And that begins by allowing them to elect their own steering committee.

We've found that in most cases young people make wise choices when electing steering committee members. Several years ago Thom was tempted to tamper with the ballot box in a steering committee election. Jane (not her real name), an overweight, homely, socially clumsy member of the group, had been nominated. Thom knew she would make a great steering committee representative. She was hard-working, reliable and really motivated to serve the group. But she had never been elected to anything in her life. And now she was running against more attractive kids who were well-liked by everyone. After the votes were cast, Thom hovered over the kids counting the ballots. He was tempted to slip in a few extra votes for Jane. But he didn't need to. The group saw Jane's good qualities too. She was elected!

Adult helpers can help the group make good decisions when electing a steering committee. Before taking nominations, take time to make several introductory comments:

1. Mention that the election is not a popularity contest. A steering committee position requires a lot of work and dedication.

2. Explain the role and responsibilities of the steering committee.

3. Suggest that the group nominate and elect only those members who will use good judgment and who will work hard.

4. Reassure young people that it's okay to nominate themselves.

Now it's time to ask for nominations. Begin by requesting that those who wish to, nominate themselves.

This strategy takes away some of the hesitancy to self-nominate, because everyone is encouraged to do so before any other nominations are posted. Usually, those who nominate themselves are highly motivated to work hard for the group.

Then open nominations to others. Categorize the nominations according to high school class.

Now you're ready for the election. If your group is large, you may ask the young people to vote for one or two representatives from their class only. If your group is small, you might ask each member to vote for one sophomore, one junior and one senior. Mention that it's okay for people to vote for themselves. Incidentally, only the young people—not the adult helpers—should vote.

Always conduct such elections by secret ballot. This is not the time for shortcuts. We know a youth worker who attempted to save time by electing the steering committee by a show of hands. He sent all the nominees out of the room and conducted the election. The results were quite surprising, because one-half of the electorate was denied the opportunity to vote; they were standing out in the hall! Hard feelings festered because those who lost found out who voted against them.

The time and trouble involved in secret-ballot voting is always worth it when people's feelings are involved.

We recommend using one young person and one adult helper to count the ballots. This method removes people's suspicions and limits knowledge of the numerical outcome to just two people. When announcing winners, simply name who will sit on the new steering committee. Do not reveal the number of votes each candidate received. That would serve no purpose but to unnecessarily injure feelings.

Meeting With the Committee

Most youth-based ministry steering committees meet every three or four weeks. A new steering committee may meet every week or every two weeks to get plans rolling.

Your designated adult helper should prepare a complete agenda for each steering committee meeting. See a sample agenda, Chart 13. The adult helper also chairs the meetings and keeps them moving.

CHART 13
Sample Agenda for a Steering Committee Meeting

1. Opening prayer. **Bob.** (2 minutes.)
2. Community-builder. **Angie.** (5 minutes.)
3. Approve minutes of last meeting. Dick. (5 minutes.)
4. Evaluation of previous month's activities. Joani. (15 minutes.)
   a. The meetings.
   b. Swim party.
   c. Canned food collection drive.
5. New business. Thom. (40 minutes.)
   a. Brainstorm fund raisers for summer trip.
   b. Decide registration deadline for trip.
   c. Choose strategy for attracting inactive members.
6. Closing circle. Sue. (2 minutes.)
7. Adjourn (no later than 8 p.m.!)

Following an opening prayer, start each committee meeting with community-building activities. This is time well-spent. Your members will feel more comfortable with one another and will feel freer to share their views. Unity and enthusiasm for the youth ministry will build.

We encourage showing steering committee members how much you appreciate their hard work. Add a special touch of love to your meetings from time to time. Conduct your meetings over a nice dinner; or take your committee members on special outings. Let them know they're important people.

Evaluation

Each steering committee meeting should include a time for evaluating recent youth ministry happenings. Refer to your ministry's goals and objectives. Are these being met by your current activities?

Take time to clothe your steering committee in affirmation. During your evaluation time, celebrate even the little steps of progress and the smallest of successes. Your committee members will thrive on this affirmation, and their energies will be renewed. Plus, we've discovered that affirmation-giving is contagious. The young people on our current steering committee now affirm one another during our evaluation time. "Rick, that was a great session on stress you led last week," one of the kids may say. Another may say, "Chinh, your closing prayer was really good." Affirmation builds self-esteem—and it models how to affirm others.

Evaluation also includes facing up to failure. When a failure occurs, talk openly with them about it. Some time ago, the quality of our weekly meetings deteriorated. Attendance dropped off. We asked the steering committee members how they felt things were going. "Discouraging," one of them said.

"What's wrong?" we asked.

"Too many kids aren't preparing their stuff for the meetings," they said. "And the content of the learning part has been pretty weak."

"What do you think needs to happen?" we asked.

"We need more help from the adults," they said.

That was a turning point for our steering committee. The failures caused a new appreciation for the adults' role in our youth ministry. They asked for more adult help to remind kids of their responsibilities and for more adult input in program planning.

The evaluation of failures forced the kids to seek more resources. A healthy learning experience emerged from the evaluation.

When a failure occurs, don't ignore it or try to smooth it over. Use the opportunity to probe your young people about what they might learn from the experience.

The Planning Process

The steering committee plans and schedules all youth group meetings, activities, retreats and special events. Often the nitty-gritty planning and preparation of youth group functions are delegated to individuals or task forces. But the steering committee coordinates the calendar and makes any necessary assignments.

How far in advance should a steering committee plan? We've found it workable to plan weekly meetings about three months in advance. Big events such as trips and retreats require a year of advance planning.

During steering committee planning sessions, adult helpers play an essential role. They come prepared with ideas and resources. This is a key element to the success of youth-based ministry. Please read carefully the following paragraphs.

We've seen adults begin planning meetings by asking the young people, "Okay kids, what do you want to do next month?" Typically, the kids remain silent and stare blankly at the adults. Those adults later wring their hands and say, "You can't leave it up to kids to plan anything. They have no idea what they want to do!"

It's not that young people don't know what they want to do. They just don't know what the possibilities are. They haven't been around long enough to build a reservoir of experience from which to draw. Abruptly asking a kid to sit down and plan next month's youth ministry calendar is like asking you to list the first 25 settings you'd make on the control panel of a spaceship. What would you say? Because you lack the necessary experience, you'd probably remain silent.

So, the secret to youth-based ministry planning is not found in the question, "What do you want to do?" It's more likely found in the question, "Which of these options do you like?"

One of the reasons we recommend that an adult prepare the agenda for steering committee meetings is to allow the adult time to gather ideas and resources for agenda items. Before we lead a steering committee planning session, we know, for example, that the group will discuss topics for upcoming youth group meetings. Knowing that, we come armed with a stack of resources. We review with the committee the current needs of young people in the group. From this list of needs the committee chooses which topics should be addressed in the upcoming weeks. We then break the committee members into pairs and ask them to choose meeting designs from the resources we brought. This process works beautifully! The kids are not stymied in frustration wondering what to do. Instead, they're proud of their accomplishments through their own decision-making.

Let's look at the golden guidelines for adults who help kids plan:

1. Come prepared to planning sessions with ideas, options and resources for each agenda item. If you're discussing fund-raising projects, for example, come to the meeting with four or five good fund-raising ideas. If you're discussing the spring retreat, come prepared with several location options and several different theme ideas.

2. Present the options and encourage the young people to add to the list with their own ideas.

3. Ask the kids to list pros and cons for each idea.

4. Do not campaign for your favorite idea. You may suggest advantages and disadvantages, but the committee never should feel that you're really invested in one idea. If they do, it may color their decision-making. If they like you, they may vote for an idea that they otherwise would have vetoed. If they don't like you, they may vote against an idea just because it's yours. In youth-based ministry, young people should feel free to make up their own minds.

5. Once the options have been presented, and pros and cons have been explored, ask the young people for their decision. (You'll find more information on youth decision-making in Chapter 11.)

After the steering committee makes its plans, ask one or more of the members to make a calendar of upcoming months. This calendar then may be copied and distributed to all youth group members—active and inactive. Encourage your young calendar-makers to be creative and have some fun. In addition to noting the important youth ministry events on the calendar, have the kids add some zany, trivial things on other dates throughout the month. See the sample calendar on the next page to give you a few ideas for your own.

Sample Youth Ministry Planning Calendar

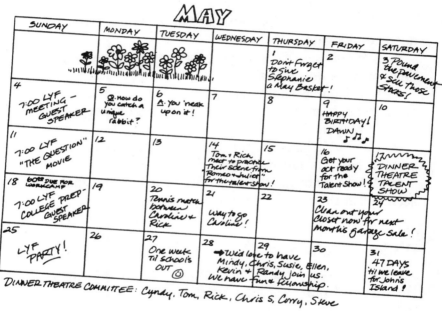

MAY

SUNDAY	MONDAY	TUESDAY	WEDNESDAY	THURSDAY	FRIDAY	SATURDAY
				1 Don't forget to give Stephanie a May Basket!	2	3 Pound the pavement & sell those stars!
4 7:00 LYF — MEETING — GUEST SPEAKER	5 Q. How do you catch a unique rabbit?	6 A. You 'neak up on it!	7	8	9 HAPPY BIRTHDAY! DAWN ♪♫♪	10
11 7:00 LYF "THE QUESTION" MOVIE	12	13	14 Tom & Rich meet to practice their scene from "Romeo & Julie" for the talent show!	15	16 Get your act ready for the Talent Show!	17 DINNER THEATRE TALENT SHOW
18 60¢ DUE FOR WORKCAMP 7:00 LYF COLLEGE PREP-GUEST SPEAKER	19	20 Tennis match between Caroline & Rick	21 Way to go Caroline!	22	23 Clean out your closet now for next month's garage sale!	24
25 LYF PARTY!	26	27 One week til school's out ☺	28	29 →We'd love to have Mindy, Chris, Susie, Ellen, Kevin & Randy join us. We have fun & fellowship.	30	31 47 DAYS til we leave for John's Island !

DINNER THEATRE COMMITTEE: Cyndy, Tom, Rick, Chris S, Corry, Steve

Delegating Beyond the Steering Committee

Young people on steering committees often are hesitant to call other members and delegate duties. To them it seems like "ordering around" their peers. So, instead of delegating, they may decide it's more comfortable to do all the work themselves.

But delegation of duties must happen to build a healthy youth-based ministry. Without a wider distribution of responsibilities, the steering committee winds up doing too much, getting burned out, and denying the rest of the youth group the opportunity to become involved. A ministry is youth-based when all the young people take responsibility, not just the steering committee youth.

Here are some tips to encourage delegation:

► Frequently remind the steering committee of the need to delegate.

► Suggest specific young people to whom responsibilities could be delegated.

► Use sign-up sheets at youth group meetings to solicit volunteers who would be interested in helping with various responsibilities.

► Use adult helpers to make verification calls to kids who've been assigned tasks.

► Ask parents for their help in verifying that their kids accomplish their assigned responsibilities.

Policy Decisions

Seventeen-year-old Brian came to us with a request. He wanted to know if his new friend Andy could go on the youth group's upcoming workcamp trip. It was a week before the trip, and the registration deadline had passed three months ago. "I really think the trip would do Andy a lot of good," Brian said. But how would Andy being allowed to go at the last minute affect the rest of the kids who had worked hard the preceding eight months raising funds for the trip?

We told Brian that the steering committee would need to make a judgment in Andy's case.

Should the steering committee make such policy decisions? We believe so. Young people are surprisingly capable in such circumstances. And they need to feel ownership in such decisions that directly affect them. Some other examples of policy decisions appropriate for steering committee discussion:

► When do freshmen or sophomores enter the group? At the beginning of summer or at the beginning of the school year?

► How much should each member be asked to pay toward the summer trip?

► What if a member doesn't participate in all the required fund raisers?

Adult helpers can help young people grapple with these types of decisions by presenting various options. For example, in Andy's case, we offered the steering committee these options:

a. Andy may come as the group's guest.

b. Andy may come if he pays the $100 fee that each youth group member paid.

c. Andy may come if he pays $100 plus another $250 as compensation for the fund-raising projects that he did not help with.

d. Andy is told that he missed the deadline and cannot come on the trip.

Then, the adult helpers must insist that the young people discuss the pros and cons of each option. In Andy's case, we asked the steering committee some tough questions. What is the purpose of our trip? How does that purpose fit Brian's desire to invite his friend? What might Andy gain from the experience? Can he afford to pay the registration fee? Should the group look for other funding if he can't? What risk is involved by introducing a new person into the group at this late date? How will the rest of the group feel? How will Andy fit into a group that has been working on unity and community-building for the past eight months? What precedent would be set by allowing him to come on the trip? What if we have five or six kids next year who try to get in at the last moment? How will Brian feel if we don't let Andy go?

Once again, adult helpers must refrain from campaigning for specific policy decisions. That was difficult for us in Andy's case. We had seen too many trips soured by the addition of a new member right before departure. But we let the steering committee make the decision. They decided to allow Andy to make the trip if he would pay $100.

Some policy decisions will result in failure. But remember, failures in youth-based ministry turn into great learning experiences for the young people. Such was the case with Brian's friend. He was a disaster on the trip. Because he had not experienced the careful community-building prior to the trip, he had a hard time fitting in. He grew resentful and began picking fights with some of the kids. Eventually, he simply withdrew from the rest of the kids, despite their Good Samaritan efforts to befriend him. By the end of the trip, even Brian wished Andy had stayed home.

After we returned home, the steering committee met to evaluate the trip. "How do you feel about your decision to allow Andy to go on the trip?" we asked. They all agreed it had been the wrong decision. "We should have stuck with our deadline," one of them said. "But, you know, I'm really proud of how the group handled Andy. I think we showed Christian love, even though the guy acted like a jerk. I think we all really learned a lot from this whole thing."

Preparing Choices for the Youth Group

The steering committee makes dozens of decisions that shape the face of the youth ministry. But the entire youth group should be involved in decision-making on any big issues that affect everyone. Some examples of such decisions: a new name for the group, the destination of the big summer trip, the recipient of the group's annual mission offering, conduct expectations for retreats and trips.

Though such issues come before the entire youth group, the steering committee does significant advance work. The committee saves the youth group valuable time by researching the issues, discussing pros and cons, and narrowing down choices to a workable list of options from which the group may choose.

For example, each year our steering committee prepares a list of possible destinations for our annual summer trip. The list may look like the one in Chart 14.

CHART 14
Summer Trip Options

1. **Trip or Activity:** Canoe trip to the Boundary Waters.
   Purpose: To build community and spiritual growth among members.
   Pros: Fun, different from last year, lower cost, could be less than a week.
   Cons: Not everyone likes to canoe and camp, seems frivolous, congregation may not support it.

2. **Trip or Activity:** Workcamp in West Virginia.
   Purpose: To help people in need, to give our group a sense of mission.
   Pros: Meaningful project, congregation will support it, enriching experience.
   Cons: A lot of work, higher cost, longer travel distance.

3. **Trip or Activity:** Choir trip to California.
   Purpose: To present musical to underprivileged children.
   Pros: Brings message of hope to disadvantaged kids, enables our group to perform, side trip to Disneyland.
   Cons: Higher cost, not everyone is involved in the musical, risk that few children would show up for performances.

When these choices are presented to the group, the steering committee also could show any available audio-visuals, brochures or handouts on each option.

The steering committee serves the total group by doing the legwork before important decisions are made.

Discipline Matters

Let's face it. No matter how fine a youth ministry may be, certain kids will misbehave. Sometimes they misbehave in such a way as to endanger themselves, other kids or the whole program. And the byproduct of misbehavior is usually discipline.

Discipline is the touchy, unpleasant side of youth ministry. Discipline often alienates adults from kids. Inflicted emotional wounds are sometimes slow to heal.

Youth-based ministry offers several ways to soften the blow often felt by disciplinary action. The young people can handle many of these problems themselves! We've found they're amazingly fair and wise in such matters.

First, the steering committee needs to create a list of behavior guidelines and expectations. Different lists may be necessary for various group activities. Then the steering committee takes these guidelines to the whole group for approval. Reasons for each rule are discussed. Young people begin to see these guidelines as aids to success rather than restrictions of freedom. When they vote to accept the guidelines, they accept ownership of them, which means they're more likely to abide by them.

Then, before any special activity such as a trip or lock-in, young people are asked to sign a covenant, pledging their agreement to follow the rules. Chart 15 is a sample covenant.

The use of covenants has a positive effect on young people's behavior. The expectations are clear and the for-

CHART 15
Covenant for the Fall Retreat

I, _____, as a member of the First
Church Youth Fellowship, agree to conduct myself according to
Christian standards during the Fall Retreat, October 12-14, at
Lake Wiki Wiki. I agree to abide by the following expectations and
rules.

1. Attend all scheduled sessions.
2. No males allowed in the female cabins; no females allowed
in the male cabins.
3. No use of alcohol, illegal drugs or fireworks during the
retreat.
4. Everyone in assigned cabins with lights out from 11:30 p.m.
to 6 a.m.

I realize that these guidelines have been established to make
this retreat the best possible Christian experience for all involved.
Therefore, I understand that if I do not abide by these expectations, I may be removed from the retreat and sent home in the
care of my parents.

_____

(Signature)   (Date)

mal promise and signature tend to modify behavior in a
positive way. And, the penalty for disregarding the guidelines is known in advance.

So, what happens if a young person breaks the covenant? In most cases, the steering committee can handle
it. Let us cite an example. Several years ago, Ron, a
member of Thom's youth group, broke the rules while
on a workcamp trip. He disappeared one afternoon while
the rest of the kids continued to work on their renovation
projects. He returned to the group a little tipsy and finally
admitted that he had been drinking with some local
teenagers.

The adults decided to take this infraction to the steering committee. The committee heard Ron's account of the incident, then excused him to deliberate its response. The adults urged the committee members to examine the pros and cons of every disciplinary option available to them. The young people took into consideration that Ron came from a rough family situation and that the trip up until this point seemed to be having a positive effect upon him. They believed Ron desperately needed the Christian influence the trip provided. They sensed that he was sincerely remorseful for breaking the rules.

So, the committee told Ron he would not be sent home. But he was told that one more infraction of any kind would mean he'd be on the next plane home. One of the steering committee members said, "We forgive you, Ron. And we love you. We want to give you a fresh start. Please don't disappoint us."

Ron didn't say a word. He simply stood, walked to the committee members and quietly hugged each one.

Ron made no more trouble on the rest of the trip. His confrontation with his peers in the steering committee was a turning point. And it was an unforgettable moment for the committee members too. A few months after the trip, Ron drowned in a flash flood.

Steering committees can perform remarkably well with many disciplinary problems. However, they should not be called upon to handle certain situations. Anytime a kid's behavior endangers himself or others, adult helpers should step in immediately with appropriate disciplinary action. Steering committees also should not be asked to deal with highly sensitive matters such as a boy and girl who are caught in bed together.

When dealing with disciplinary problems, always caution the steering committee members to use their utmost maturity. This includes maintaining confidentiality about

Acknowledgments

We thank all the young people and adults who have been our willing partners in our adventure of granting big doses of responsibility to kids.

Joani thanks the people of Trinity Lutheran Church, Hudson, Wisconsin, who believed in her while she helped them do more than they thought they could do.

Thom thanks John Shaw for his instrumental role in developing this philosophy of youth ministry during the early '70s.

And we thank Dan and Cindy Hansen for their encouragement and openness during our latest involvement in this form of youth ministry.

More Practical Programming Resources from

Group®

Do It! Active Learning in Youth Ministry
by Thom and Joani Schultz

Learn how to actively involve your teenagers in group meetings and activities with creative, non-lecture programming. Learn to design simple, fun programs that your group members will look forward to ... and remember afterward. Plus, you'll get 24 complete, faith-building programs.

6×9 paperback, 144 pages
ISBN 0-931529-94-8
$9.95

Youth-Led Meetings
by Dr. Elaine Clanton Harpine

You'll use these 10 powerful meeting plans to help your young people develop important leadership skills. Kids will learn how to accept responsibility, make decisions and work better with others. Includes meeting outlines, checklists and handouts, along with a special training retreat for your kids.

8½ ×11 paperback, 120 pages
ISBN 0-931529-53-0
$12.95

More Creative Resources from *Group*

Developing Youth As Leaders video

Help your teenagers become Christlike leaders. Your kids will identify, discuss and practice leadership skills in activity-packed programs. Train your kids in 5 meetings, a weekend retreat or a one-day intensive session. You'll guide their progress with complete, easy-to-follow instructions in the 71-page users guide. Plus, you get ready-to-copy handouts.

98-minute VHS video kit
ISBN 0-931529-44-1
$69.95

Youth Ministry Cargo
by Joani Schultz and dozens of contributors

Discover how you can use simple, everyday stuff to teach unforgettable object lessons about peace, poverty, self-image, forgiveness and more. Over 240 creative program ideas using low- or no-cost materials you can find at church or right in your own home.

7×10 paperback, 405 pages
ISBN 0-931529-14-X
$9.95

Training Teenagers for Peer Ministry
by Dr. Barbara B. Varenhorst
with Lee Sparks

Train your young people to apply their Christian faith to care for and support friends. Equip your young people to deal with typical teenage issues: family problems, death and dying, substance abuse, suicide and sexual concerns. Offer peer ministry training to your group.

6×9 paperback, 154 pages
ISBN 0-931529-23-9
$8.95

any young person involved.

Adult helpers should report disciplinary problems to the appropriate people back home such as parents and the senior pastor. This action heads off rumors and interprets any corrective action taken. During a retreat, 15-year-old Bobby noticed that his wallet was missing. Our steering committee decided to take a calm approach to the problem, since Bobby wasn't sure if the wallet dropped out somewhere along the road or if someone in the group stole it. We questioned each of the kids who shared Bobby's room at the retreat. We were convinced that none of them took the wallet.

We thought all would be quickly forgotten. After all, the wallet contained only $10. But within 48 hours of our return home, Thom received a call from the chairman of the congregation, who also happened to be Bobby's father. He screamed into the phone with boiling anger, "What kind of riffraff have you allowed into that youth group? A bunch of thieves? Why didn't you come down on those kids?"

"What do you think we should have done?" Thom asked.

"You should have strip-searched them! You're too soft!" He was too angry to hear our account of the happenings. He ended the conversation with, "I'm going to do everything in my power to see that you're relieved of your duties here!" He eventually was successful.

We learned a hard lesson. Immediately upon our return from the retreat, we should have notified the parents and the senior pastor of the missing wallet caper and why we chose to handle it as we did. Instead, Bobby got to everyone first, changed his story, and portrayed the youth group as a pack of thieves.

Problem Issues in the Group

Youth-based ministry allows you and your adult helpers to step back and look at the big picture. When doing this, if you see a trouble spot, take it to the steering committee for consideration. For instance, if you notice cliques beginning to strangle the youth group, bring this dilemma to the steering committee.

Years ago we brought the problem of waning attendance to the steering committee. Together we came up with a plan to address the problem. We phoned parents of kids who had dropped out. We told them that we would be by on the next Sunday night to "kidnap" their kids for a special youth group meeting. We asked that they keep their kids home, but not tell them we were coming. We then rented a gorilla costume, put it on one of our bigger guys, and visited the inactive kids' homes. The gorilla ran inside the houses, found the kidnapees and carried them (usually kicking and screaming) to our church bus waiting at the curb.

The steering committee's solution to our attendance problem was well received by everyone, especially the kidnapees, who tried to explain their ordeal to their disbelieving friends at school the next day.

Kids' Inaction and Irresponsibility

Don't be surprised when steering committee members, or other youth, show signs of irresponsibility. Expect it. They're kids—not adults. They will forget. They will fail to prepare. They will disappear just when they're needed most.

Be patient, and know that your young people are no different from kids in any other church. They all "blow it" from time to time.

When kids fumble a responsibility, don't ignore it. Talk

with them. Be honest about your disappointment. But
don't condescend. They're still learning about responsibility and independence. They need to know you'll still
love them even if they disappoint you. It's that bond of
love that will make them try harder next time. If they
sense your love and the love of the group, they'll eventually dread the thought of disappointing you or them.

Avoid disappointments by building an airtight verification
system. Use your adult helpers to systematically contact
each kid with any kind of responsibility. Accept this work
as an ongoing necessity to your ministry's success.

And, finally, focus on the good things. Don't allow the
kids' irresponsibility to discolor all the positive things that
are happening. A year ago our spirits were low after a
steering committee meeting. Just as we were lamenting
some of our kids' irresponsibility, Chinh showed us a
project she undertook on her own, with no adult prodding
whatsoever. She researched, assembled and copied a new
comprehensive roster of all active and inactive members—
something we really needed.

Believe in your kids. They'll disappoint you sometimes.
But many other times they'll make you proud.

Unsuitable Responsibilities for the Committee

Youth-based ministry does not advocate relinquishing
all youth ministry responsibilities to the young people.
Clearly, adults need to handle a variety of sensitive matters. Some examples:

► **Selection and dismissal of adult helpers.** As
we've mentioned before, these types of personnel matters need the attention of a small group of adults—the
administrative team.

► **Confidential problems with young people.**

Adults with counseling skills need to handle serious
problems such as kids suffering with alcoholic parents.
   ▶ **Representation on church boards or councils.**
Some people argue with us on this one. But, in most
cases, we don't believe young people should be asked
to serve on congregation-wide legislative bodies. The purpose of youth ministry representation on such boards
should be to win approval of youth ministry items before
the board. Many adult board members view young people
on such boards as "cute" rather than capable or persua-
sive. Yes, representation on the board may give a kid
some experience. But it's not unlike asking a teenager to
represent you as a defense attorney in a criminal case.
Certainly the kid would get good courtroom experience,
but is it worth the price? Besides, church board meetings
are frequently boring and less organized than the kids'
steering committee meetings. Why discourage your
teenagers before they're old enough to make a real difference in congregational matters?
   Although the steering committee does not handle everything, it does "steer" the youth ministry by making plans
and policies, and referring big decisions to the whole
youth group.

CHAPTER TEN

Involving Parents in Youth-Based Ministry

Parents are partners in the success of youth-based ministry. Their support, or lack of it, often determines the level of growth their kids will experience in the youth ministry.

In the past, many youth workers viewed parents almost as obstacles to their youth ministries. We heard statements such as, "Parents? Are you kidding? I spend all my time trying to undo the damage they've done to their kids! I see myself as a counterbalancing force, trying to give these kids the love they're not getting at home."

Thankfully, that antagonistic attitude seems to be disappearing. It's being replaced by a spirit of cooperation. Youth workers today recognize that their influence on young people is small compared to the parents'. The family, not the youth worker, wields the real power in shaping young lives. Admitting this fact frees youth workers to use the family structure as a prime element in youth ministry.

Good youth ministry means family ministry. If a youth ministry is to be truly effective, it must find ways to assist families.

Parenting is one of the most important, crucial jobs anyone ever tackles. But it's also one of the few jobs in which no one receives any real training. Parents are thrust into their positions and expected to just "find their way."

People in youth ministry can offer support and resources to parents. This results in a double benefit. First, the parents will likely do a better job of parenting and developing good Christian kids. Plus, they'll likely view the youth ministry as a positive force in their families, and will therefore be more eager to support it.

Youth-based ministry really needs parental understanding and support. If kids sense the encouragement of their parents, they'll be more inclined to take their youth-based responsibilities seriously.

Parents Meetings

Parents need to understand the philosophy and mechanics of youth-based ministry. Since this form of youth ministry is easily misunderstood, parental education is essential.

Before you launch your new youth-based ministry, schedule a parents meeting. Explain the goals and objectives of the new ministry. Consider using your teenage planning task force members to make at least part of the presentation. This offers the parents a glimpse of youth-based ministry in action.

Don't expect all of the parents to embrace youth-based

ministry with enthusiasm. During an introductory parents meeting at our church, a mom expressed her doubt that youth-based ministry would work. "This all sounds good. But I don't know how you think it'll ever fly," she said. "I remember the youth ministry we had here several years ago. Now *that* was really good. I can't see how you're going to be able to match that."

That comment dropped a haze of disappointment and skepticism over our meeting. But we ventured ahead with our plans. A year later that same mom pulled Joani aside after Sunday morning worship and said, "I just want you to know how pleased I am about what's happening with the youth program. John (her son) is so excited! He's really growing and getting a lot out of it. I want to thank you."

Plan to meet with parents at least twice a year. Give them updates on youth ministry happenings and goals. Enlist their support and their help on specific projects.

And, take time to carefully explain any recent youth-based ministry failures. Reinforce the youth-based concept that young people often learn more from their failures than from their successes. Point out positive outgrowths from particular failures. Help parents see the value of granting young people the freedom to fail. Some parents may even pick up on this idea and try it within their own families.

Be sure to also plan a parents meeting prior to any youth group trip. This offers an opportunity to explain the purpose of the trip and to distribute itineraries. Parental release forms also may be signed at this time.

Mailings to Parents

Good youth ministries recognize the benefit of building and using a mailing list of parents of active and inactive youth. Regular mailings can inform parents of upcoming youth events and remind them of their key role in the success of the youth ministry.

Many successful youth ministries publish a monthly newsletter especially for parents. This offers the opportunity to include brief parenting tips. Such tips can be found in books, newspapers and magazines. Parents love concise articles on topics such as communicating better with teenagers, understanding typical adolescent behaviors, recognizing signs of teenage depression and suicidal tendencies, establishing family spiritual growth times, disciplining, and so on.

Mailings may be created by the key youth worker or by a designated volunteer adult helper.

Maintaining written contact with your kids' parents will help win their love and support.

Parent Support Groups

Your youth ministry program can provide a very simple but meaningful service to families through parent support groups.

Many parents bear great anxiety because they think they're the only ones facing a particular problem with their kids. They find real relief and solutions when they get together with their peers—other parents of adolescents.

But many parents are sheepish about initiating "bull sessions" with other parents. They need someone to organize a support group for them. Your youth ministry team can provide a valuable service by organizing parents into small support groups that meet regularly, usually monthly. This requires very little effort. Set up times and places and invite the parents. Perhaps you'll want to provide a moderator and a simple agenda.

Helping parents help one another strengthens families—
and youth ministries.

Involving Parents as Youth Ministry Helpers

As we stated in Chapter 7, we do not recommend using
members' parents as regular adult helpers in youth-based
ministry. However, parents can and should be asked to
help with special tasks such as:

✔ driving for special events such as concerts or
progressive dinners.

✔ helping in the kitchen for snack suppers.

✔ being resource people for certain topical studies.
(For example, for a health-related study, use parents who
are physicians.)

✔ serving as members of special task forces such as
food planning for a camping trip.

There are hundreds of ways to involve parents in
youth-based ministry. Involving them properly will en-
hance the ministry and work toward building stronger
family relationships.

Parent/Youth Nights

From time to time we like to invite selected parents
to a regular youth group meeting. This allows them the
opportunity to see, firsthand, how youth-based ministry
works. It's especially effective with parents who may
have criticized or misunderstood the youth ministry. Prior
to attending a meeting they may have said, "I don't think
my kid is getting anything out of the youth group," or,
"I think you're just being lazy by turning the group over
to the kids to run." Complaints often turn into compliments when parents see youth-based ministry in action.

To further build parent understanding and to encourage

healthy family relationships, ask your steering committee to consider planning adult/youth nights from time to time. Research, by Search Institute and several others, shows that today's young people yearn for closer bonds with their parents. Both kids and parents are struggling to find meaningful ways to communicate with one another. Parent/youth nights can provide a wonderful service by setting up forums for good communication.

Have some fun and bridge the generation gap at the same time. Set up role plays of common parent-teenager dilemmas such as a kid who comes home an hour after curfew time, or parents who don't like their teenager's friends. Reverse roles: Ask a parent to play the role of a teenager, and vice versa. This provides a time for fun and laughter—and deep insight when discussed afterward in small groups.

At the end of the evening, pass out copies of "Table Talk" (see Charts 16 and 17) to each family to take home with them. Joani produced this resource to help parents and their teenage children to further their communication at home. This fun tool can break old patterns of communication and help start new ones. "Table Talk" is designed for use at the table during family mealtimes. Parents and young people ask questions from their "menu" selections and make special discoveries about one another.

Events such as parent/youth nights and resources such as "Table Talk" have made a positive effect in our families' lives. They illustrate how youth workers can reach out to families as a whole. Such efforts respect and lift up the home as the primary setting for youth ministry.

CHART 16

Parent's Menu

A Fine Assortment of Questions to Ask Your Teenager

HOW TO USE "TABLE TALK"

These "Table Talk" menus happen to be "conversation menus"; they're meant to help you make new discoveries about each other. You're free to select and ask questions from any section. You can use the menus again and again for listening and finding out more about your family members. "Table Talk" promises to bring a new and exciting perspective to your relationship.

But before beginning, there's one important rule: The person who asks the questions must *listen.* No arguments, defensiveness, put-downs or shouting allowed. Just listening and understanding. (Remember, this is "Table Talk," not "Family Fight"!)

So go ahead. Ask the questions and see what course your conversation takes!

Appetizers

Ask: What's your favorite and tell me why.

- ✔ your favorite time of the day
- ✔ your favorite room in the house
- ✔ your favorite subject in school
- ✔ your favorite food
- ✔ your favorite kind of music

Soups 'n' Salads

Ask: When was the last time you felt . . .

✔ glad?	✔ thankful?
✔ mad?	✔ pressured?
✔ confused?	✔ content?
✔ embarrassed?	✔ hurt?

Á La Carte

Read Ephesians 4:2: "Be always humble, gentle, and patient. Show your love by being tolerant with one another."

What quality is most important to our relationship—humbleness, gentleness, patience or tolerance? Why?

Together decide practical ways to show these qualities of love to one another.

The Main Course

Ask: What item on the table best describes your feelings about . . .

- your friends?
- your family?
- your grades?
- your church?
- dating?
- your parents?
- work?

- your home?
- your choice of clothes and hairstyle?
- yourself?
- your faith?
- your choice of music?

(Don't forget to have your teenager explain why!)

Dessert

Complete one or more of these sentences:

- Our most memorable family meal together was . . .
- Three things I really appreciate about my parent(s) are . . .
- What I enjoy most about my family is . . .
- What I need most from my parent(s) right now is . . .
- One thing I'd really like to say is . . .

CHART 17
Teenager's Menu
A Fine Assortment of Questions to Ask Your Parent(s)

HOW TO USE "TABLE TALK"

These "Table Talk" menus happen to be "conversation menus"; they're meant to help you make new discoveries about each other. You're free to select and ask questions from any section. You can use the menus again and again for listening and finding out more about your family members. "Table Talk" promises to bring a new and exciting perspective to your relationship.

But before beginning, there's one important rule: The person who asks the questions must *listen.* No arguments, defensiveness, put-downs or shouting allowed. Just listening and understanding. (Remember, this is "Table Talk," not "Family Fight"!)

So go ahead. Ask the questions and see what course your conversation takes!

Appetizers

Ask: What's your favorite and tell me why.

✔ your favorite day of the week

✔ your favorite time of the year

✔ your favorite way to relax

✔ your favorite place to visit

✔ your favorite sport

Soups 'n' Salads

Ask: When was the last time you felt . . .

✔ happy?	✔ angry?
✔ discouraged?	✔ put down?
✔ satisfied?	✔ pressured?
✔ zany?	✔ carefree?

Á La Carte

Read James 1:19: ". . . Everyone must be quick to listen, but slow to speak and slow to become angry."

What makes this verse difficult to follow? What could we do to make it easier?

Together devise a specific plan to put this verse into action in your communication.

The Main Course

Ask: What item on the table best describes your feelings about . . .

- right now?
- your work?
- your friends?
- your child(ren)?
- your expectations of me?
- church involvement?

- family relationships?
- God?
- the future?
- the past?
- the present?
- being a parent?

(Make sure your mom or dad gives reasons for answers.)

Dessert

Complete one or more of these sentences:

- I wish we'd be able to . . .
- Three qualities I really admire in my teenager are . . .
- I'm really proud of my teenager when . . .
- If I could be alone with my teenager for one whole day, I'd like to . . .
- One thing I need from my teenager right now is . . .

CHAPTER ELEVEN

Equipping Youth With Decision-Making Skills

E nabling young people to weigh alternatives and
make their own decisions is a centerpiece of
youth-based ministry. At first, kids often are amazed
and impressed that they've been granted such power
and responsibility.

And, the decision-making skills they're taught in a
youth-based ministry will go with them for the rest of
their lives. They will be equipped to tackle the tough
moral dilemmas they are sure to face in school, college
and on the job—when their parents, the youth worker and
the pastor are nowhere in sight.

Young people can build their decision-making skills with
all kinds of youth ministry issues. All major decisions that
affect everyone should be brought to the entire youth
group. Some examples:

- Type and destination of the summer trip.
- Election of steering committee members.
- Rules and guidelines for retreats.
- Large expenditures of group funds.

Presenting the Issues

The group decision-making process begins with the steering committee presenting various options. As we stated earlier, the steering committee can save the youth group valuable time by researching, discussing and preparing options to present to the entire group.

Adult helpers play an important role when the youth group weighs decisions. Here's where finesse is required to help kids decide—without deciding for them. Prior to each decision, adult helpers should make sure the discussion touches several milestones:

■ **Examine pros and cons of multiple options.** Adults should gently guide the discussion to make sure the group looks at advantages and disadvantages of each possible course of action. This can be accomplished through well-timed probes such as, ''That idea sounds like it has a lot of advantages. But what are some possible dangers with it? What if everything doesn't go as planned?'' By prodding young people to look at all sides, adults teach fairness, informed judgment and evaluation. Imagine how this influence will impact kids' decisions later in life!

■ **Forecast possible outcomes and consequences.** Adolescents live in the ''now.'' They often make short-sighted decisions based on how they'd be affected today with no thought of the decision's impact on tomorrow. Adults can help teenagers grow out of this tendency by encouraging kids to forecast. When options are presented, adults should ask questions such as,

"What effect would this decision have on us three months from now? a year from now? What precedent would we be setting by this decision? How will others view this decision?"

■ **Review relevant Christian principles.** If the young people themselves do not bring appropriate Christian truths into a discussion, adults may do so. But this is not the time for "proof-texting." Adults can do more damage than good by quoting miscellaneous scriptures out of context. Let's look at a positive example of introducing Christian principles in a discussion. Terry dropped out of the group during the time most of its fund-raising projects were conducted for the summer trip. Then, a couple of months before the trip, he came back. He realized he needed the group more than he thought. He asked to be allowed to go on the trip, even though he missed most of the fund raisers. During the group discussion of this matter, an adult read the story of the Prodigal Son and asked, "Does this story apply to our situation with Terry?" A great discussion followed. Terry was welcomed back into the group and allowed to go on the trip. And the kids learned something about relating God's Word to their everyday lives.

■ **Assure that all opinions are aired.** Most youth groups have a couple of young people who are outspoken. Sometimes these kids are natural leader-types who may disproportionately sway youth group opinion by their self-confident "selling" of particular positions. One such kid is Barry, a past member of our youth group. He was a great kid—articulate, intelligent, enthusiastic, committed, a leader at school. Whenever a group discussion began, everyone looked at Barry. He spoke and the other kids nodded. Most decisions went Barry's way. Aware adults can minimize this tendency by eliciting responses from a variety of kids. When possible, call on each young person

for his or her opinion. If you have a Barry, start with
someone other than him. His opinion, when mixed with
other viewpoints, will then take less prominence.

■ **Summarize.** After the group dissects the options,
adult helpers should review what has been said. For example, if your group is trying to decide between visiting
nursing home residents on Christmas Day or making gifts
for orphanage kids, you might say, "I heard you say the
old folks really appreciate our Christmas visits, but that
other youth groups in town are planning to do that this
year too. And you said that nobody ever helps the or-
phans, but that making good gifts would take a lot of time
and money." Adults must resist the temptation to bias
their summarizations. Vigilant self-discipline must be used
to dispassionately review the young people's views without slipping in any editorializing. Even a simple adjective
can betray impartiality. Fair and thorough summarization
leads to better decision-making—and teaches young
people the lifelong skill of summarizing all the pros and
cons before making a decision.

Adult helpers should feel free to share their input prior
to group decision-making. However, campaigning or rail-
roading by adults has no place in youth-based ministry.
Here again, finesse makes the difference between ramrodding an idea and sharing an idea. Let's look at an
example. This concerns the choice of a fund-raising
project:

THE RAMRODDING APPROACH: "Not another car
wash! Last time we did that I got soaking wet in your
stupid water fights and almost caught pneumonia. Besides, we only made $30. And the adults did most of the
work!"

THE SHARING APPROACH: "We might want to take
another look at how the last car wash went. I believe we
took in $30. How do you think that compares with other

fund raisers we might do? And last year I think only four young people showed up. Why do you suppose that was? How do you think it might be different this year?''

Notice how the adult in the sharing approach example added to the discussion without being pushy or biased.

Making the Decision

Several different methods may be used to help the group make its decisions. Choosing the appropriate method should be done with care. Adult helpers may need to step in and ask that the group use a particular method, to guard against unfairness and hurt feelings. Here's a look at each method.

■ **Consensus.** This is a wonderful choice for many decisions. It works especially well in smaller groups. Through discussion and compromise, group members work to find a solution that everyone can accept. This process usually requires more time, but it's often worth it. Group unity blossoms when everyone feels good about a group decision. However, consensus won't work with every decision, because sometimes compromises can't be found that please everyone.

■ **Voice or hand vote.** This method works well when there's little potential for hard feelings about the outcome of the vote. It's a fast and clear form of decision-making. Use voice or hand voting for smaller, more arbitrary decisions such as choosing dates for the fall retreat, or selecting a color to paint the youth room. If certain well-respected, outspoken kids attempt to steer group opinion, don't use a voice or hand vote. And never use this method for big decisions or elections of youth representatives.

■ **Secret ballot.** This is a sure, reliable method of decision-making. The written, confidential aspect signals

to young people the significance of their vote. It's a
slower method, but it's often justified. Use secret ballots
for elections of youth representatives, for decisions on
sensitive issues, and anytime kids may feel undue pressure from other kids (or adults) to vote a certain way.
The kids in our group were deciding between two mission
trips—one to South Carolina, the other to Mexico. The
vocal kids all favored Mexico. We adults were quite
confident the majority wanted to go to Mexico. But we
noticed many kids seemed quiet about their opinions. We
asked for a secret ballot vote. The winner: South Carolina. This was a classic example of a "silent majority."
Had that decision been made by a hand or voice vote, we
are convinced the pressures from the vocal kids would
have sent the group to Mexico.

Teaching Life Skills

The decision-making process in youth-based ministry
isn't simply good youth ministry. It's something much
bigger than that. It's teaching young people big skills that
they'll use the rest of their lives.

Many churches try and fail to tell kids what to decide.
"Don't listen to that type of music!" "Don't support
the arms race!" Some young people may temporarily
follow the passionate advice of a youth worker. But
almost all young people reach the stage in their adolescent development when they question and discard the
legalistic rhetoric of authority-types.

Youth-based ministry teaches young people *how* to
decide—using their learned skills of evaluation, analysis of
options, forecast of consequences, review of Christian
principles, counsel with peers and summarization. Thus,
when they're out on their own, far from their family and
home congregation, they're equipped to make wise Chris-

tian decisions.

You may ask, "Does all of that really seep into the kids involved in youth-based ministry?" We continue to hear evidence that it does. Brian was a member of Thom's group several years ago. He went on to college, graduated, married and set out on his adult life. His mother pulled Thom aside one Sunday and said, "I want to thank you for all you did for Brian. You taught him how to think through things, and how to make up his mind as a Christian young man. He still talks about that youth group and what he learned. He's doing great now."

CHAPTER TWELVE

Ingredients for Good Youth-Based Meetings

"For where two or three come together in my name, I am there with them" (Matthew 18:20). And whenever your group gets together, it's important to structure your meetings to make the most of the Spirit's presence. This chapter shows you how.

After grappling with the purpose of weekly get-togethers, the young people on our planning task force designed a meeting structure with seven critical components:

1. Community-builders,
2. Music,
3. The "learning part,"
4. Refreshments,
5. Prayer,
6. Affirmation,
7. Closing.

We were impressed with our kids' list of essential ingredients. So, we'd like to pass them along to you. With these seven ingredients your group can reflect a youth-based, scripture-based focus for ministry. By purposefully stirring together these ingredients your young people and adults consistently will experience a fun, caring community of believers. Much like the early church: "They spent their time in learning from the apostles, taking part in the fellowship, and sharing in the fellowship meals and the prayers" (Acts 2:42).

Use the following guidelines and ideas to develop your own quality programs that meet your kids' needs. But don't forget the youth-based ministry philosophy. Involve kids. Use young people to plan and lead each ingredient. They can do it! The variety of ingredients capitalizes on your young people's diversified gifts. Plus, teenagers learn how to be leaders.

Involving kids as leaders doesn't eliminate the vital role of adults. Adults are needed to act as guides, to supply resources and to offer ideas. When teenagers are in the leadership spotlight, an adult facilitator can keep things moving throughout the meeting by a subtle nod of the head, a glance that says to move on, or by making a statement such as, "Pat, you're next." All of these provide support and keep the meeting moving. One of the pleasures of youth-based ministry comes when others say, "Wow! Those kids led the whole meeting! And it went so smoothly!" Adults will smile knowing their role as "behind-the-scenes meeting movers" didn't overpower the kids' visibility as leaders.

Before digging deeper into the details of each ingredient it's important to appreciate the investment that is needed. Quality meetings take work. And that involves dreaming, planning, double-checking, doing, evaluating. But it's worth it. Just think of the impact that 90 minutes of quality programming can have on kids! Making the most and the best use of your time together shows you value teenagers' time (and your own time). Building a relationship with God deserves the best you can give.

Once your steering committee selects a theme for a meeting, the meeting ingredients can be planned in detail. Your steering committee may ask different young people to prepare each ingredient. If your group is small, one young person may take the responsibility for a particular ingredient for a month or so. If your group is large, responsibilities for ingredients may rotate among kids every week.

Remember to supply resources to your young people to help them plan their meeting ingredients. Share with them the ideas in this chapter and the resources listed at the end of the chapter.

Let's look at combining these seven ingredients in a youth-based meeting. They can be arranged in any order, depending on the meeting's theme. Meetings can vary in length, but a 90-minute unit is a good, workable time frame.

There's nothing magical about the seven meeting ingredients, but with the Spirit's help, a magical transformation can occur in your youth group. Pray that it will.

Ingredient 1: Community-Builders

Community-builders aren't new to youth ministry. Most people feel pretty comfortable using mixers and games, yet many fail to look at the reason and rationale for this ingredient.

When planning community-builders for your group, think possibilities: high-, medium- or low-energy games, get-acquainted activities, name tags, discussion starters. Use whatever gets participants interacting with one another. Community-builders aren't passive. And they're not one-person shows or skits by comic youth workers; everyone should get into the act.

Community-builders should be fun, structured times for building and strengthening friendships. Don't be fooled. Close-knit youth groups don't just happen—it takes time to build relationships.

"But we always have the same five kids," you say. Great! There's always something new to learn about each other. The thrill of God's creative plan ensures that we're always a new creation with new insights to share. "When anyone is joined to Christ, he is a new being; the old is gone, the new has come" (2 Corinthians 5:17). Besides, why not have a positive attitude and prepare for the big day when someone brings a visitor?

There are hundreds of community-building ideas floating around the world of youth ministry. In your search for resources, keep a few rules in mind for constructive community-builders:

● **Build group unity.** Whether you choose a game or a discussion activity, the community-builder should create a sense of oneness and promote positive feelings. There's no room in youth-based ministry for practical jokes at someone else's expense.

The old funnel-in-the-pants, pour-water-when-they're-not-looking gag reeks of laughing at someone's misfortune. Disguising an onion as a caramel apple is another nasty trick to pull on the poor kid who's trying to win the caramel-apple-eating contest. So is the secretly wired chair that sends a jolt of electricity to zap the unsuspecting victim when he gives a wrong answer. The list goes on and on. Tragically, some youth workers get a bang out of having a laugh at someone else's expense. "But it's okay if *I'm* the brunt of the practical joke," say some adults. What difference does it make who the victim is? What are we teaching our young people? That we should revel in others' misfortune? Is that good Christian education?

● **Boost kids' self-esteem.** Youth-based ministry is founded on the belief that teenagers are gifted, special, important members of the body of Christ. Everything we do should point to their uniqueness. Kids live in a media-blitzed culture that blares out messages such as, "You're not good enough—not pretty, talented, athletic, sexy, rich or smart enough!" The church must do its part to counteract the world's bleak messages. We can help kids see their value. "But you are the chosen race, the King's priests, the holy nation, God's own people, chosen to proclaim the wonderful acts of God, who called you from the darkness into his own marvelous light" (1 Peter 2:9).

Yet some youth workers continue to subject kids to mixers and games that assassinate self-esteem. We once observed an adult who stood before a crowd of teenagers and shouted, "Now shake hands with someone who's uglier than you are!" He chuckled—we cringed.

Not all games and mixers are so obviously degrading. Others are more subtle. Resist activities that put kids on the spot. Beware of requiring a special skill or ability. When your kids are first getting to know each other, don't ask them to tell about something too personal. It's too threatening. And avoid incorporating physical attributes into games and mixers. For example, a game as simple as "line up from tallest to shortest" can be excruciating for a self-conscious young girl who towers over her peers, or for a short, insecure boy. A supposedly harmless game meant for fun can pierce fragile self-images.

● **Provide for appropriate touch.** Choose community-builders that incorporate a comfortable level of touch. Backrubs, handshakes, hugs and games that create a non-threatening time for touch help quench kids' need for physical closeness.

Make certain that physical activities are positive and not uncomfortable. Sure, there'll always be kids who aren't well-acquainted with touch, but that doesn't lessen their need for it. Adding group hugs, holding hands during prayer time or giving quick backrubs all help make closeness accessible.

Involving Youth in Community-Builders

Encourage optimum youth involvement by supplying community-building resources and ideas for the kids. Then let them pick and choose. Offer guidance in selecting games and mixers that are uniquely appropriate for your group.

Resist the temptation to use adults to lead community-builders all the time. Let the kids do it! They may need your coaching and encouragement. Saying, "You can do it," will pay off.

You can make their job easier with some crowd control. An adult voice saying, "Come on everybody, let's get started," often helps the group focus on what's about to happen.

Kids at first might not always be the most articulate instruction-givers. But as they grow as leaders, they also grow in confidence and self-esteem. Soft-spoken Laura enjoyed planning and leading games. At first her directions came out jumbled and unclear. But as time went on (and with practice), Laura got braver and better. Her peers grew to respect her and her self-image blossomed.

Community-Builder Ideas

Here's a selection of community-building activities to

get you started. Feel free to adapt these to your own situation.

● **Pinky Link.** Use this game to create a spirit of play, to help group members get acquainted and to experience non-threatening touch.

Have group members practice "linking their pinkies" by asking them to "shake hands with each other's little fingers." Then ask them to follow any instructions given by the leader. For example, when the leader says, "Link a pinky with someone who's wearing blue jeans," everyone should locate someone with jeans and interlock little fingers. The leader will call out a different instruction each time, and group members must find new pinky-link partners. Keep the game moving. Kids can link with more than one person's pinky at a time.

Here are some link suggestions. Link a pinky with someone who . . .

- was born the same month as you were.
- has the same number of letters in his or her first name as you do.
- is wearing a ring.
- likes hamburgers more than pizza.
- is wearing the same color as you are.
- has no shoelaces.
- has a phone number with "5" as the last digit.
- plays the piano.

● **Describe Your Day.** Use this discussion starter to get participants in touch with each other's feelings.

If your group is larger than 10, form smaller groups. Have participants sit in a circle with their feet toward the center so everyone can see each other's shoes. Begin with the person with the biggest smile and move to the left. Have each person select a shoe from the circle that best represents his or her day and tell why. If two people choose the same shoe, that's okay.

Use tnis as a time to bring the group together, to listen to one another's frustrations and good news.

Be creative in adapting this exercise. You can use objects other than shoes. You could choose something in the room, an article of clothing, a color, a sound. Tangible things can be used to help describe intangible things such as feelings or faith. Or, ask kids to describe something other than their day—their relationships with their families, or with God, for instance. You might choose a question that relates to the meeting's theme.

● **Mini/Mega Mingle.** Use this name tag activity to promote sharing among group members.

Give each person a piece of paper and a colored marker. Have group members write their names on each side of the paper by drawing "mini" letters on one side and "mega" letters on the other. Then ask them to write five things on the "mini" side they wish they had "less of." For example, homework, zits, responsibilities at home. On the "mega" side they should write five things they wish they had "more of." For instance, money, time with a best friend, albums. When everyone is finished writing, the group should stand and get ready for the Mini/Mega Mingle. Have a leader shout out the words "mini" or "mega." When players hear "mega," they must instantly find partners, face each other and share what is on the "mega" side of their name tags, and tell why they chose the things they did. Allow about 30 seconds per sharing time. Then shout "mini" or "mega" again.

Group members must always find a new partner. Continue the game until the kids have a chance to share with at least five or six others. Then stop. Ask: "What did you learn about yourself? about your values? about the others in the group? What surprised you most? Which category, mini or mega, was most difficult to decide? Why?"

To add some spice, play lively background music throughout the sharing. Create a mingling party atmosphere.

Ingredient 2: Music

Teenagers' lives revolve around music, like a record revolves on a turntable. So it's important that we don't underestimate music's power. Even if you have kids who won't sing or who think singing is dumb, it's important to offer music to your group each time you meet. Music can do so many positive things. Here are a few noteworthy reasons to use music:

● **Music builds group unity.** Singing creates a bond, a climate of togetherness. Make certain you *include* kids, not *exclude* them. Singing the old favorites—songs the long-time members know—may alienate new group members and visitors. Our kids solved this problem by buying songbooks for everyone. Now, newcomers feel included. Also, looking at songbooks eases some of the self-consciousness of hesitant singers. (Remember, unauthorized copying of music or lyrics is illegal. You must either purchase songbooks for everyone or obtain written permission from the publisher to copy. Even transferring lyrics to transparencies or slides without permission is against the law.)

● **Music provides a focus.** Besides the obvious unifying fact that everyone is doing the same thing, music points everyone in the same direction. Music can focus on the meeting's theme; it can reinforce learning; it can teach scripture; it can be used for prayer.

To make the most of music's focus, plan songs ahead of time. Have kids who plan the meeting choose appropriate songs that will underline the theme. Let music move

the group toward a goal. Yet, it's important to be flexible
in your meetings. Sometimes the group's spirit will need
energizing, sometimes it will need mellowing.

● **Music sets the mood, the atmosphere.** Take
advantage of the power of song. If you want the group to
settle into a devotional mind-set, don't lead into the meeting with a rip-snortin' action song. Or, if you want to
energize the kids, a solemn chorus of "Just As I Am"
won't work.

You can positively and carefully alter the group's mood.
Use high-energy songs with actions, shouts and clapping
to build a fun, electric feeling. Worshipful, more mellow
tunes can precede discussions or prayer times. Upbeat
recorded music, playing as group members arrive, sets
the tone of: "Hey, something's happening here! This is
gonna be fun!" Soft, instrumental background music
works great for reflective moments or for small group discussion times. The background music helps to drown
out neighboring small groups and creates a more non-
threatening atmosphere. It also covers uncomfortable gaps
in conversation.

● **Music uses young people's talents.** In keeping
with youth-based ministry philosophy, music can heighten
kids' involvement. Whether teenagers are singing or
providing accompaniment, they're showcasing their gifts.
Teenagers like to see other teenagers in the spotlight.
We're always amazed at the interest and affirmation kids
give other kids when it comes to music. So often an
abandoned guitar at a retreat finds its way into a young
person's hand. Then, before long, other kids gather
around the minstrel.

Young people don't need to be polished musicians, but
they can help lead singing. Not long ago, two guys in our
youth group decided to learn to play the guitar. For starters, each learned a different chord. Then, as a team, they

alternated chords for our group singing. They had a great time.

Involving Youth in Music

Have young people choose the songs. Have them pass out the songbooks. Encourage your musical-types to play their guitars, flutes, pianos, tambourines and kazoos. Even if you're the only guitar or piano player in the group, ask a team of young people to stand with you to lead songs.

If no one in your group plays an instrument, use sing-along tapes. Perhaps your young people could invite their musical friends to the meetings to help with the music.

When you use pre-meeting recorded music, ask one or two young people to be the "deejays." They can supply the cassette player and select the music. This is a great way to involve your shy teenagers.

Invite young people to prepare a song to share with the entire group. It wouldn't be a performance as much as a sharing of talent. Solos and duets offer a change of pace from group singing.

Finally, think of innovative ways to involve all group members during the singing: actions, clapping, snapping fingers, dance steps, addition of "instruments" such as jingling keys, clapping shoes together, slapping the floor or chair backs, and so on.

Music Ideas

Here are a few ways to involve your group using music.

● **New words—old tunes.** Use this idea to tailor-make your own songs and to build teamwork.

Divide group members into "tune" teams of three or

four. Give each team a sheet of newsprint, a marker and
a familiar tune. For example, use "Mary Had a Little
Lamb," "Old MacDonald Had a Farm," "Amazing
Grace," "How Great Thou Art," "Are You Sleeping?"
and "Row, Row, Row Your Boat." Ask each team to
write new words to the old songs. You might want to
suggest song topics. For example, they could write songs
about the youth group, the theme of the meeting or the
upcoming retreat, prayers of thanksgiving, whatever. Allow 10 to 15 minutes for composing and for writing the
words on newsprint so everyone can see them. Have
each group share their song creations together and have
fun! Rounds are especially fun because they create har-
mony without being musically difficult.

If appropriate, save the songs for future get-togethers.
A few years ago, Joani worked with some young people
at a summer camp who created new meal prayers, and
put them to the music of familiar rounds. The words were
written on posterboard, decorated and used for meal
prayers year-round at the camp. It was fun to return to
the camp, sing the special prayers and know that other
campers were enjoying the creations.

● **Name songs.** Use your own ingenuity to personal-
ize songs, using the names of people in your group. Hunt
for familiar tunes that lend themselves to adding group
members' names.

Personalizing music creates a special sense of community, builds self-esteem (we all like to hear our names),
and helps people learn each other's names.

In one of Joani's youth groups, the kids adopted the
song "Jesus in the Morning" as a "name" ritual. The
song uses repetitive words: "Jesus, Jesus, Jesus in the
morning, Jesus at the noontime. Jesus, Jesus, Jesus when
the sun goes down." Every time the word "Jesus" appeared, we put in a group member's name. So, it went

like this: "Brenda, Kim, Sherry in the morning. Brian at the noontime. Joel, Andy, Dana when the sun goes down."

Other songs that would work for names include "Love (name) Lifted Me," "Oh, How I (we) Love Jesus (name)," "Thank You, Lord, for Giving Us Life (name)."

● **Air bands.** Use recorded music to provide a chance for "non-singer" kids to get involved. Air bands allow everyone to be a "star" for a moment.

Choose a popular song or contemporary Christian song to play while group members "lip-sync" the words. Have kids form "bands" with members who "sing" and play imaginary guitars, drums and keyboards. All they do is act out the song as if they were actually performing. No sounds from the band members allowed.

By using air bands, you can incorporate high quality contemporary music into your meetings. Kids love to act out the songs, and it's fun to watch too!

Ingredient 3: The Learning Part

The "learning part." We wish we could claim responsibility for such a descriptive title. But we can't. Our planning task force grappled with a name that included Bible studies, discussion groups, speakers, films, simulation games—anything that promotes faith growth. Soft-spoken 16-year-old Debbie jumped in. "How about calling it the 'learning part'?" she suggested. And it stuck.

When planning this "meat" of your meeting, use these guidelines:

● **Zero in on three youth ministry learning methods:** relational, wholistic and experiential.

Relational means that learning rarely happens in isolation. Kids need to interact and bounce around ideas with other members of Christ's body. God's impact on their lives needs to be seen as a reflection of their relationship with God and with one another.

Wholistic learning includes issues and concerns that are relevant to kids' diverse needs. Congregations make a monumental mistake when they separate God and the Bible from the rest of life. Kids need to see what difference God makes at school, home, work and play. A wholistic learning approach courageously tackles the tough stuff of day-to-day living and decision-making.

Experiential learning involves doing. People learn best by doing, by getting personally involved. For the Gospel message to sink in, we need to bring it to life. Passive listening to a 20-minute sermon or lecture is probably one of the poorest forms of education, particularly for today's young people. But when you get them involved— speaking, singing, reading, playing, interacting, moving, touching, sniffing, hearing—they're more apt to remember what's being taught. Think about this: Which of the following would you be more likely to remember? Someone's lecture about baking cookies, or your actual involvement in the kitchen—mixing the batter, rolling the dough, using the oven and smelling the aroma. The *experience* etches the subject being taught in your mind.

● **Use small groups.** Youth-based ministry believes in the power of group process. Even more, it believes in the power of the Holy Spirit at work in young people. Too many youth workers think kids learn only when wise adults verbally pour their insight and knowledge into teenagers. That's not true. Kids can learn from each other too. They need time to process what they've experienced. And that happens most effectively in small groups. No more than eight people should make up a small group. If you have more than eight, form smaller

groups. In this way, each person gets a chance to participate if he or she desires. Small groups provide comfort
and security to people who normally might hold back.
Encourage each small group member to share. But
remember, participants always reserve the right to pass
if they don't feel comfortable sharing.

● **Provide need-meeting opportunities.** Learning
times should blend faith and life. Whatever you do must
meet kids' needs. Resist the temptation to deal only with
topics you, as an adult, feel comfortable with. Beware of
irrelevant or shallow programming that doesn't connect
scripture to life. Challenge kids. Tackle controversial
issues. Wrestle with problems that don't have easy answers. The church must be a safe haven where teenagers
can ask hard questions (Is abortion always wrong? If God
is loving, why is my mom dying of cancer?). It also must
be a place where they discover how God's Word inter-
sects with *all* of life.

Involving Youth in the Learning Part

The learning part could be the most difficult ingredient
to put together. But don't let that scare you or the kids
who will lead it. Young people possess a certain power
when they present topics and faith issues to their peers.
Plus, kids who prepare and lead the learning part gain so
much: self-confidence, a deeper understanding of the
topic, an outlet for exercising their faith, affirmation from
their peers. So, use teenagers to plan, prepare and
present the learning part. You can be essential to their
success by providing creative resources, ideas and support. Take advantage of the resource bibliography at the
end of this chapter.

Even if you feel your kids might not be ready for such
leadership responsibility, ease them into ownership by al-

lowing them to choose topics. Poll the group to identify interesting topics. Ask teenage planners to select weekly topics from the top vote-getters in the survey.

If you or other adults lead the learning part, remember the value of involving the kids. Use simulation games, experiences that relate to the topic, small group discussions, large group feedback sessions. Stretch yourself as a planner by always including individual involvement and group interaction. Remember: Everyone learns best by doing.

Learning Part Ideas

Here's a selection of learning part ideas to get you started. Add, subtract and adapt to fit your young people's needs.

● **Old Life/New Life.** Bring to life Colossians 3:8-14 with this scripture experience.

Ask kids to sit in circles of four or five persons. Give each small group a Bible, a newspaper, markers and blank address label stickers. Ask participants to read Colossians 3:8-9. Ask members to take a sheet of newspaper and write (in large letters) some aspect of their lives they wish to get rid of. For example: anger, greed, hurt, jealousy, revenge. When everyone is finished, ask the small group members to tell each other what they wrote and why. Then, to "get rid of these things," have them crumple the papers and toss them over their shoulders.

Continue by reading Colossians 3:10-14. Explain that it's now time to "put on the new self." Ask kids to take a label sticker for each person in their small group. For example, if there are three other kids, each person in that group should take three stickers. Each person then chooses a quality from Colossians 3:12-14 (compassion, kindness, humility, gentleness, patience, tolerance, forgiveness, love) that best describes each person in the circle. They write the respective qualities on the stickers. Then they tell which quality they've chosen for each person and then stick the labels on the appropriate people.

Conclude with each small group joining hands and reading Colossians 3:12-14 again.

● **Anger Awareness.** Use this activity to discuss how anger affects people's lives.

Ask each group member to find and face a partner. Explain that the purpose of this activity is to explore what happens when people get angry. For a "practice run," ask participants to shout the opposite of whatever the leader says. For example, if the leader says, "yes," they say, "no," five times in a row. If the leader says, "right," they say, "wrong," five times. Once the group understands the opposite shout, add another dimension. Begin by speaking softly and gradually speak louder, then softly again. Practice that.

Next, have partners conduct their own shouting matches. But, abide by this rule: No one may use "you" or "I." Let them experience the shouts, trading off who starts. They may use any opposites they choose: young/old, big/little, black/white, boy/girl, stop/go, and so on.

The room will be filled with noisy, angry sounding people. After a few minutes of chaos, ask partners to join another pair to form a foursome. Have them discuss: How did you feel during this activity? What relationships did the shouting matches remind you of? Why is anger so dangerous?

Select a volunteer to read Proverbs 15:1 and Ephesians 4:26. Discuss: What do these verses teach about anger? How can you keep anger from leading you into sin? What happens if you stay angry all day? What are positive ways to handle anger?

● **Excuses, Excuses.** Let this game lead into a discussion about excuses that keep us from living a full Christian life.

Bring the group together in a circle. Ask a volunteer to read Matthew 22:1-6. Explain that they're going to play an "excuses" game. Beginning with the person whose name begins with "A" or the closest letter, go around the circle to the left. The beginning person must make up an excuse that begins with the letter "A." For example: "I can't come to the wedding feast because I have *athlete's foot*." The next person might continue by saying, "I can't come to the wedding feast because I have *athlete's foot* and *band practice*." Each person repeats all previous excuses and adds another excuse that begins with the next letter of the alphabet.

When you've completed the alphabet, have a volunteer read Matthew 22:7-14. Form discussion groups of six to eight. Discuss: What did you learn about excuses during the game? When do you usually make excuses? What does Jesus mean by this parable? What excuses do people use to avoid living a full Christian life? How can you say "yes" to the Christian faith without using excuses?

Ingredient 4: Food

All 25 of them hunched over two long tables. They obviously were enjoying themselves. The entire youth had just dived into the mega-sundae we built in a long plastic rain gutter. The atmosphere was filled with fun, fellowship and good feelings. That's what food can do. It builds community.

Jesus knew what eating together could create—oneness, community, sharing. Christians have chosen to remember Jesus with a cross, which is certainly an important symbol. However, Jesus asked to be remembered by something else: ". . . the Lord Jesus, on the night he was betrayed, took a piece of bread, gave thanks to God, broke it, and said, 'This is my body, which is for you. Do this in memory of me . . . This cup is God's new covenant, sealed with my blood. Whenever you drink it, do so in memory of me' " (1 Corinthians 11:23-25). Our Lord chose food and drink, things that become a part of us, to remind us of his ultimate sacrifice. Eating together stirs up a special bond among those who partake. So, use refreshments and meals to create community.

Incorporate food into youth group meetings for another reason: People *like* to eat. Treats can be considered gimmicks of sorts—but they work. If offering chocolate cupcakes gets more kids to fill out a survey—offer them! If preparing snack suppers before meetings brings kids together—prepare them!

Some leaders might groan and say, "One more detail to plan. And it seems so frivolous and unnecessary!" Go to the extra trouble. Think of food as one relatively simple, non-threatening way to involve kids. Not only can they eat, but they can bring food and prepare it too. This is another way to involve parents too.

Use food creatively, for more than satisfying hunger. Let it reinforce the learning part. (Didn't Jesus do just that in the feeding of the 5,000?) One group of ambitious devotion planners always looked for snacks that would underline the message in the lesson. For a self-image devotion using Kermit the Frog's song, "It Ain't Easy Being Green," Michelle baked a batch of green chocolate chip cookies. Another devotion centered around shoes. Members were to choose a shoe that best represented their relationship with God. After everyone shared, Joel passed around a can of shoestring potatoes. Treats become an innovative way to add to the learning experience.

Involving Youth in Food

Besides being the recipients of treats, young people can organize who will bring food, what will be offered and how it will be served. For example, Jean may decide ice cream would be a fun snack. But she also wants to reinforce teamwork, so she decides kids should feed each other the ice cream.

Let young people have fun tying food into the theme. If you're studying Jesus, the Bread of Life, a natural choice for refreshments would be homemade bread. You'll be amazed at the fun kids will have dreaming up creative treats.

Food Ideas

Here's a "menu" of fun foods for youth groups. Taste test some of these.

● **Pizzas With Personality.** Provide ingredients for pizzas and use pizza-making as a community-builder.

Form "pizza groups" of two or three. Give each group pizza dough, a pan, tomato sauce and toppings. Ask the groups to form their dough into a shape that best describes their group. Maybe they'll decorate the pizza like a football because they play football; or a butterfly because they're celebrating Easter. Have groups explain their pizza creations. Then bake them and enjoy eating them.

For another dimension, award prizes for the most descriptive, the most creative or the craziest creation.

● **Teamwork Taffy.** Use candy to create a spirit of cooperation and to reinforce learning.

Plan a meeting around the theme of handling sticky situations. After the learning part, prepare taffy ingredients and host an old-fashioned taffy pull. Not only will the candy reinforce the meeting's learning part, but it will also build community. Encourage kids to think of ways the taffy represents sticky situations in their lives.

● **Fortune Cookie Fun.** Have a volunteer group of kids make fortune cookies and fill them with group-building messages. The messages might be words of affirmation for specific group members. For each person, make three or four cookies with messages such as, "Jody, you're always willing to listen," "We know we can count on Jody as a friend," etc. Pass them out during the affirmation portion of the meeting.

Or, you could split messages among different cookies. Then kids hunt for other kids who hold the other portions of their messages. Split song titles such as "Mary Had a/Little Lamb," or famous pairs such as "Samson/Delilah," or words such as "valen/tine." Have kids break open their cookies and link up with their other halves. To form larger groups, divide up by categories (such as all famous pairs together) or have cookie messages divided into fourths such as "spring/summer/fall/winter."

Or, put Bible verses in the cookies.

Ingredient 5: Affirmation

Affirmation: the reinforcing of the positive in people. This ingredient holds wonderful power. If your group becomes serious about affirmation, this one aspect of your ministry could transform your group. Your attendance may increase. Group unity will soar. Self-esteem will skyrocket. Why is affirmation so crucial? Because young people are bombarded with put-downs from their peers, in school, in sports, and from the media. They hear the messages that say they're inadequate and they don't measure up. Don't let the world control teenagers' self-images. Actively step in and promote God's idea about his precious creations. Kids long for a positive voice—God's voice—that says, "You're okay. I love you."

Affirmation can have a profound effect on your young people. Eric was a neat kid. Energetic. Kind. Giving. But he was like everybody else: He'd get down on himself. The youth group gave him hope. "I don't know what I'd do without the support of the group," he said. "All week at school I feel like I get run-down. But after youth group, I feel like my batteries get recharged. I can face another week. I wouldn't miss youth group for anything!" The power of encouragement. It gives kids the strength they need to face the stresses and struggles of this time in their lives.

Affirmation is not only great to receive, it's great to give too. Use it to teach teenagers to be graceful, grateful receivers of praise. How many times do you hear kids negate compliments by denying them or laughing them off? Group members can learn how to be gracious receivers. They also can get wrapped up in the joy of giving. It's always more fun to dish out the good stuff instead of the put-downs. Affirmation can bring a special element of love to your group.

Never leave this portion out of your meetings because you can't think of anything creative to do. Positive words and actions can be simple. A one-word praise or a thank-you (spoken or written) can have as great an impact as a lengthy speech. So can a quick hug or a comforting pat on the back. Sometimes, let affirmation take the form of prayer—a circle prayer of thanks for the person on your right, or an exchange of names for prayer partners. Use spoken, written or non-verbal tokens of appreciation—a "strength bombardment" spoken to each group member as he or she stands in the center of the circle; a poster for each member passed around the group for everyone to add words of affirmation; friendly, non-verbal actions toward members such as a fluff of the hair, a crazy hand-shake, a hug.

Another hint: Be vulnerable as an adult. Set an "en-courager" example. Kids will watch how you accept praise. If you graciously, humbly say, "thank you," recognizing God's special gift of you and gifts in you, kids will pick up on that attitude. They also will absorb your example of giving appreciation. Your sense of humor can be positive, not cutting. Your freedom in expressing care will show them how to do it.

Don't underestimate how special your affirmation time can be. You can bet that kids save and savor every tidbit of positive feedback they receive. We've seen yellowed, crumpled sheets of paper from an affirmation activity taped to kids' bathroom mirrors. We've noticed "good qualities" name tags stuffed in kids' Bibles and journals. Teenagers will treasure those reminders. And so will adult helpers!

Involving Youth in Affirmation

Have group members dream up new and clever ways of making each other feel good. They'll be in touch with the greatest needs. For example, if the local high school is entrenched in the state championships, kids might be prompted to design individual trophies for each other. Or maybe it's semester test time, and they want to give "A's" for certain friendship qualities in each of the members.

Another affirmation activity might be triggered by a tragedy. For example, a classmate's unexpected death could bring the group together in prayer, thanking God for each individual's support and for each person's life being so important. That may sound like an extreme ex-ample, but it's that close contact with kids' immediate life-experiences that pours relevance into your meetings.

Most of all, make sure every young person in the group is a giver and receiver of encouragement. You might even want to use kids as specially appointed "care-givers." For instance, if your group has a loner or an outcast-type, match a "care-giver" to that person who will make sure the loner feels welcome, included and affirmed.

Affirmation Ideas

Here's a sampler of ideas to help your group members become good affirmers.

● **Credit Cards.** Have fun with this activity that helps kids give credit where credit is due!

Give each group member a piece of paper the size of a credit card with his or her name written across the center. For an added touch, decorate it like a credit card with a series of numbers along the bottom, a globe or whatever symbol might best represent that person.

Have group members sit in a circle. If your group is larger than eight, form smaller groups. Ask members to pass their "credit cards" to the person on their left. In small but legible writing have kids write on the back of the card what they'd give the cardholder person credit for. The responses must all be positive. For example, on Patti's card someone might write, "I'd give Patti credit for being so patient with me," or "I'd give Patti credit for helping clean up the youth room last week."

When the credit cards return to the original owners, have members read them. Encourage everyone to keep the credit cards in their wallets as reminders that God gives them credit for being unique, valuable, special people.

● **Invisible Gift Giving.** Play this game to have fun giving imaginary gifts.

Have group members form a circle. If your group is larger than 10, form smaller groups. Explain that everyone gets a chance to give invisible gifts to each other. It's an opportunity for them to use their imaginations and forget about what the gifts cost. Anything is possible. But there is one rule: The gifts must reflect something you appreciate about the other group members. And, there's an added dimension. Each gift-giver tosses the invisible gift to the recipient. The recipient must catch the gift, then "reshape" it and toss a new gift to another group member. People should make sure each person receives a gift at least once.

Here's how it goes. Jane says, "I'd like to give Bonnie earmuffs because she's such a great listener." Jane tosses Bonnie the imaginary earmuffs. Then Bonnie says, "I'm giving Chuck a tuxedo because he's such a classy kind of guy!" Chuck then catches the invisible tuxedo and continues sending presents.

● **Group Thanksgiving.** Use this affirmation exercise to build up the group's spirit of togetherness.

Form a circle, with group members putting their arms around each other's waists. Begin by having kids move to the right as a circle "dance." Designate one person as the starter. That person shouts, "Thanks, group!" (Or add your group's name.) When the group members hear those words, they stop. The person who shouted says what he or she really appreciates about the group. "You all make me feel so welcome and included." The person must conclude with, "Thanks, group!" Those words set the circle in motion again, but in the opposite direction. Then another person can shout, "Thanks, group!" The circle stops, he or she compliments the group, concludes with, "Thanks, group!" and the thanksgiving continues. The game concludes when each person has had a chance to say thanks, or when no one else shares.

Ingredient 6: Prayer

Prayer sets a youth group apart from all other groups. With prayer, the gathering of young people no longer resembles a meeting of the 4-H Club, soccer team or Spanish club. It's a group of teenagers who believe "wherever two or three are gathered in my name, I'm there."

Incorporating prayer in every get-together unleashes God's power. "Ask, and you will receive; seek and you will find; knock, and the door will be opened to you" (Matthew 7:7). Prayer opens the communication channels between God and your group members; it promotes a growing, trusting relationship with our Lord.

Be creative with your prayer times. God, the creator of creativity, invites us to use innovative ways to communicate with him. Use spoken and written prayers, sing songs, listen to music for prayer time, act out prayers, take time for silent prayers.

Avoid stuffy, wordy, canned or cliché prayers. Speak to God naturally—the way you'd talk to a close friend. Leave out the "Lord, 'just' do this . . . and 'just' do thats." Pray in today's language. "Thees," "thous" and "thines" sound stiff and archaic.

Matthew 6:7-8 makes a case for brief, to-the-point prayers: "When you pray, do not use a lot of meaningless words, as the pagans do, who think that God will hear them because their prayers are long. Do not be like them." Another advantage of brief prayers? Kids who might feel self-conscious about praying out loud will feel less threatened if they're not expected to be excessively expressive.

Probably the greatest gift prayer brings to your meeting is as a "connector." Prayer connects you with the focus and the purpose of gathering together: Jesus Christ. Plus prayer connects group members with each other. It's a beautiful opportunity for the community of believers to share joys, hurts, needs, forgiveness, quiet, hopes, praises, thanks, fears. Prayer weaves a web of support, strengthened by the Holy Spirit's power.

Involving Youth in Prayer

As an adult, resist the temptation to lead all the prayers. Chances are, you're more articulate than some of the teenagers; your flowing, lengthy prayers could inhibit young people in their prayers. A teenager might think, "I couldn't possibly pray like that! So I won't even try." So, when an adult does lead the prayer, he or she should model prayers that reflect a real person-to-person connection with God.

Obvious as it may sound, encourage young people to do the praying. Many adult leaders might lead the prayers thinking it's just easier to do themselves. Or perhaps they don't want to put the kids on the spot. Let kids pray.

Ask young people to choose prayer "themes." For example, they might decide prayers for the meeting could revolve around family, school, youth group unity, thanksgiving, affirmation, etc. Allowing kids to select a theme helps them focus on an area to pray about.

Use group members to write prayer requests for the prayer time. Maybe there are times when one person offering a corporate prayer on behalf of everyone might have a special impact. Or, designate one young person to collect prayer requests and post them on a prayer poster for all to see and pray about throughout the week. Challenge members to pray for each other throughout the week.

Ask kids in advance to be the prayer leaders. That way

they can come prepared, instead of feeling put on the spot.

Prayer Ideas

Here are a few ways of praying in your group. Give them a try!

● **One-word Prayers.** Create a comfortable non-threatening atmosphere for prayer with this idea.

Have group members form a circle and join hands. Introduce the prayer like this: "We're going to go around the circle and offer a one-word prayer. The one word can be whatever you choose. It could be 'help,' 'thanks,' 'friends,' or the name of a person. God knows what you mean. If someone else says your word, that's okay. I'll begin, and we'll go to the right. Let's pray." Pause for a moment to give kids a chance to think of their prayer word. Conclude with, "Amen."

This can be a simple, yet powerful way to pray together. It's not too scary; everyone can participate. Another time you might want to have people simply say the name of someone they'd like to pray for. We did this in a parents meeting and asked parents to say the names of their teenagers. It was a powerful and moving experience.

● **Thanks to the Right.** Build a bond of concern for group members with this form of prayer.

Have participants say a prayer of thanks for the person on their right. Read 1 Thessalonians 1:2-4 as an introduction. There's something very powerful about listening to someone talk to God on our behalf.

● **Prayer Bags.** Use this prayer idea to encourage prayer throughout the week.

Have kids each write their names on as many slips of paper as you have group members. If your group is larger than 10, form smaller prayer groups. Give each person a paper sack with his or her name printed on it. Form a circle with participants. Have group members pass their bags to the left so each person can place his or her name in the bag. When the bag returns to its owner, it should be full of names of people to pray for. In addition to these names, have kids think of others to pray for (pastor, absent group members, friends at school). Have them add those names to their bags.

Challenge kids to take their prayer bags home and draw out one name a day. They should remember that person in their prayers all day. They could even call or drop a note to that person to say they're praying for him or her.

Ingredient 7: Closing

The grand finale. The finish line. The dessert. The way a meeting ends is as important as a good first impression. A specific, identifiable "closing" wraps up the meeting in a package. Group members know their time together is over. Or, maybe the meeting's send-off is just the beginning—if you believe ministry happens in the day-to-day activities of the young people. Jesus' "closing" let the disciples know their "meeting" was over and it was time to move on: "Last of all, Jesus appeared to the eleven disciples as they were eating . . . He said to them, 'Go throughout the whole world and preach the gospel to all mankind' . . . After the Lord Jesus had talked with them, he was taken up to heaven and sat at the right side of God. The disciples went and preached everywhere, and the Lord worked with them and proved that their preaching was true by the miracles that were performed" (Mark 16:14-15; 16:19-20).

Closings are important. How many meetings have you

attended in which people started leaving—and you weren't sure everything was over? Kids who leave early, who filter out before the meeting is complete, do damage. They crumble the sense of community that was built during the meeting. Kids who "trickle out" appear to discount the value of the members who stay. A way to eliminate this unfinished, ragged edge is to make closings a ritual.

Lots of groups have developed special closing habits, or rituals. The beauty of doing the same thing each week reinforces the importance of wrapping it all up. Everyone knows the meeting is over. Examples of closing rituals could include a circle prayer time, a group hug, a circle dance with a special song, a special handshake or cheer.

One way to ensure effective closings is to end the meetings or events at a specific time. Not only will parents appreciate your promptness but so will kids who might have homework. A definite ending time helps everyone know what to expect.

Send off the group with a feeling of completion, community and affirmation. The last impression can be a lasting impression.

Involving Youth in Closings

Have a team of teenagers create a closing ritual. Let them delight in designing special endings with a flair. Maybe they can write new words to a familiar tune or invent a special dance step.

Another not-so-obvious way to involve group members is to be clear about expectations: You want *everyone* to stay for the entire meeting. Say that you value each person's contribution to the group—for the entire meeting. Promise to be out on time. Your closings will then offer an excellent exit and a reinforcement of community and a family feeling.

Closing Ideas

Here's a collection of closings for you. Use these and make up your own.

● **Victory Cheer.** Let this activity become a closing ritual for your group.

As a group, make up words and actions for a special, tailor-made, one-of-a-kind group cheer. Include rhythm claps or other cheerleading-type fun. For example, "Give me an 'F' (XX)! Give me a 'C' (XX)! Give me a 'Y' (XX)! What's that spell? First Church Youth! First Church Youth! Yeaah!'' (Hands in the center for a huddle handshake).

Use the cheer whenever you're ending a meeting. You might even want to lift one person on to the group members' shoulders and "carry away'' a different person each week—just like a victory celebration.

● **Candle Pass.** Use this as a meditative prayer closing.

Have group members sit in a circle. Light one candle and pass it to each person in the group. Whoever has the candle says a prayer of thanksgiving, help, praise, confession. Members have the freedom to pass the candle if they don't want to pray aloud. Encourage those who wish to pass, to offer a silent prayer before giving the candle to the next person.

● **Standing Ovations.** As a grand finale, celebrate each person's uniqueness.

Have group members sit in a circle. Begin by announcing who'll receive a standing ovation. For instance, call out, "Paul!'' Paul then must stand, take a bow or do whatever gracious act he'd like. All the while the other group members stand, applaud and generally make Paul feel like the most famous person they know! Then, call out another person's name and repeat the standing ovation. Move on quickly so everyone gets a chance, yet move slowly enough so each person who receives an ovation can soak it all in.

Evaluating the Meetings

One essential activity (often forgotten) is evaluation. Without looking at the positives and negatives of the meetings, you'll never know what to improve upon or what to celebrate. Ongoing evaluations can be done in a number of ways:

● **By the adult helpers.** This is a great way for the adults to give input about what's happening during the meetings. Ask all your adult helpers to meet for coffee or ice cream after each meeting. Let them summarize the meeting, how it went, what they appreciated about the kids' leadership, what could be changed. It's also a good time to discuss specific teenagers and what they might need from the adults. Let the evaluation focus on ministry, always looking to what's best for the young people.

Not only does this reveal kids' needs, it also builds camaraderie among the adult helpers.

Adults can share ways to solve problems, decide who needs to be followed-up with reminders, decide what issues need to be brought to the steering committee, and so on.

● **By the steering committee.** Using this group of evaluators keeps the ownership of fine-tuned, quality meetings with the kids. They take responsibility for successes and failures. Evaluations of meetings by the steering committee help kids focus on what they need to do to maintain quality. For example, Tom, a young person, looked back on the past few meetings led by kids. He voiced a concern. "When I try to announce something or explain a game, I feel like nobody wants to listen. We need some adults to help get everyone's attention. Maybe an adult could help with 'crowd control.' " Tom voiced a real need in the meetings. The steering committee then took action to get more adults involved who'd help with the meetings in that way.

The steering committee can share its disappointments and wrestle with solving problems. It can also celebrate the success stories of youth-based ministry.

● **By the whole youth group.** Occasionally, it's helpful to ask the entire group for feedback. This can be accomplished by written surveys. Include incomplete statements such as, "What I really like about our meetings is . . ." or, "One thing I'd like to change about our youth meetings is . . ." or, "I'd be willing to help with . . ."

With creativity, hard work and honest evaluation, your youth-based meetings can meet many needs and draw your young people closer to Christ.

Resources for Meeting Planning

For community-builders: *Try This One* series (Group Books); *Building Community in Youth Groups*, Rydberg (Group Books).

For music: *The Group Songbook* (Group Books); *Songs*, Anderson (Songs & Creations).

For the learning part: *The Giving Book*, Thompson and Schultz (John Knox Press); *Dennis Benson's Creative Bible Studies*, Benson (Group Books); *Helping Youth Interpret the Bible*, Gobbel, Gobbel and Ridenhour (John Knox Press); *Youth Group Meeting Guide*, Bimler (Group Books); *Tension Getters* series (Zondervan/Youth Specialties); *Youth Ministry Cargo*, Schultz (Group Books); *Group*

Magazine's Best Youth Group Programs (Group Books).

For affirmation: *Building Community in Youth Groups*, Rydberg (Group Books).

For prayer: *Creative Worship in Youth Ministry*, Benson (Group Books).

For closings: *The Giving Book*, Thompson and Schultz (John Knox Press); *Building Community in Youth Groups*, Rydberg (Group Books).

Epilogue

Youth-based ministry. There's nothing magical about it. And it's not easy. But our years of watching young people grow and mature through youth-based ministry have convinced us that this form of ministry uniquely fits today's young people.

We encourage you to try these concepts in your youth ministry. We cannot guarantee you overnight success. In fact, the youth-based ministry at our current church did not really begin to cruise until its second year. Then things seemed to take off. The kids accepted their responsibilities. They began to see that they were the ones who determined the quality of the program. And the quality did improve. Attendance climbed. Kids invited their friends. The summer workcamp trip was a big success. Kids' faith and commitment to Christ grew.

Word of our youth-based ministry spread. Our sister church across town called to learn our group's "secrets." Teenage members of our steering committee trekked over there to tutor their leadership team. Imagine the satisfaction our team received seeing our kids leading youth ministry workshops for another church!

We're reminded of the example of our Lord. He spent some time among us, modeling how we should conduct our lives, teaching us the principles of Christian love. Then he said, in effect, "Now, you do it. I will always stand with you. But I'm counting on you now to take the responsibility of doing my Father's work. I believe in you.''

May you too follow Christ's example, and challenge your young people by giving them real responsibility. May you believe in them, as he does.